KU-113-303

Antique Furniture

COLLINS NUTSHELL BOOKS

Antique Furniture

JOHN McDONALD

Illustrated by the Author

COLLINS
LONDON AND GLASGOW

GENERAL EDITOR: J. B. FOREMAN, M.A.

First published 1965

© *William Collins Sons & Co. Ltd., 1965*

PRINTED IN GREAT BRITAIN
BY COLLINS CLEAR-TYPE PRESS

Contents

INTRODUCTION

There are, in the great historic houses of the British Isles, some fine examples of furniture, which, when sold at an auction fetch very high prices. Recently a marquetry commode by John Cobb, cabinet-maker to George III, was sold for over £9,000 and a late 17th-century bracket clock by Thomas Tompion brought £10,000 at a sale in Edinburgh.

However, there was a great deal of furniture which was made for more ordinary people like the country doctor, the successful tradesman or the well-to-do farmer. Such furniture made in wainscot oak or fruitwood was the product of lesser cabinet-makers and country craftsmen. It was well made and durable, the purchaser saw to that, and often it was very similar to, but less ornate than, its aristocratic counterpart.

In many instances the work of the provincial cabinet-maker was of a high order, like that of the Gillows of Lancaster. At one period in the 18th century their work was so highly esteemed that they opened a warehouse in London and their goods were sent all the way there by sea. Sometimes a country craftsman might try his hand at some of the cabinet-maker's more advanced techniques and has left behind his version of a chest with a veneered front or a Chippendale style ribbon-back chair.

It is hoped that this book will help people to form a right judgment about old furniture when they see something they would like to buy. Quite often there are pieces which may have been in the reader's family for generations and it should be a simple matter to identify and date them from the illustrations and the text. It might even help the uncertain owner not to discard or sell for a song some unconsidered piece which has real va.ue.

Accordingly, this account of antique furniture has been planned, not so much as a continuous history, but by types of furniture. Such a scheme will allow the development of a particular item, where this is evident, to be traced down through the centuries.

There is no doubt that the only way to become really knowledgeable about antique furniture is to look at it again and again. Apart from owning interesting pieces, it is essential to visit museums, historic houses and antique shops where such furniture is on display. It can then be examined closely and even handled, if permission is first obtained. This little book of handy pocket size should enable the visitor to such places to find them doubly interesting. Perhaps it will foster a very rewarding study and appreciation of one of the most important of the domestic arts.

CHAPTER 1

A Summary of the Main Periods

Gothic rarities—early Tudor and Elizabethan homes—the first
Stuarts and the Commonwealth—Restoration baroque design
and the beginning of the Golden Age—continental and social
influences on fashion—William and Mary—the sober charm of
Queen Anne furniture—the long Georgian period and the century of
the great designers—French rococo style and Thomas Chippendale—
Robert Adam and the "beautiful spirit of antiquity"—honest
George Hepplewhite—poor Thomas Sheraton—Regency and Empire
vogues—Victorian quaintness and romanticism—Abbotsford furniture.

Very little domestic furniture has survived from the
Middle Ages. This was the period when the great English
castles and abbey churches were built and men lived in a
feudal society. Life was vigorous and rough and there was
little time or opportunity for practising the arts. It is only
from a few surviving examples of medieval woodwork and
from the hand-written, illustrated prayer books like the
Luttrell Psalter that we know what these Gothic tables,
chests and stools looked like.

The Middle Ages may be said to have ended with the
last battle of the Wars of the Roses in 1485. The victorious
Henry VII, first of the Tudor kings, initiated a long period
of peace which was to enable Englishmen to enjoy a more
civilised way of life. For the first time they were able to
build their houses as homes for living in and not as forti-
fied refuges against an enemy. They were able to think of
furnishing these homes with household goods which were
unlikely, any more, to be looted or broken up by the warring
soldiery. But fine furniture was not to be had at once.
This happier state of affairs did not, of course, hold good

9

for the North and the Border counties where spasmodic outbreaks of strife still prohibited a settled existence.

The few places which the struggle between the Yorkists and Lancastrians had left unscathed were the great abbeys and other religious houses. Here the arts of living had continued to develop, albeit with an essentially religious air about them. The decorative motifs, like the geometric tracery and the cusped spandrels, of the masons who built the churches were used as low relief carvings on the woodwork of the carpenter and joiner. Thus, the patterns of Gothic architecture were to be found among the earlier decorative forms used to embellish domestic furniture.

There is a well-known painting in the National Gallery, London, of Jan Arnolfini and his wife by Jan van Eyck, painted in Bruges about 1434. In it a chair with a tall back is visible at the back of the room. The chair looks more like a bishop's throne with its Gothic tracery carved in low relief on the framework and panels but it was, nevertheless, a piece of domestic furniture in the house of a well-to-do Flemish merchant.

Nearly one hundred years later, the German artist, Hans Holbein, came to England in 1526 and painted a picture of the household of Sir Thomas More, Lord Chancellor to Henry VIII. In the background is a large oak dresser with a canopy top. It is interesting to note that the fretted cresting on the top of Van Eyck's chair and the cresting of Holbein's dresser are almost identical. Apparently the Gothic style prevailed in Flanders, France and Britain throughout this time and it is conceivable that quite an amount of continental furniture was imported into England and Scotland.

The dissolution of the monasteries in the early years of the 16th century and the transfer of much monastic material to the homes of the people also did much to increase the Gothic character of the furniture in use. There is a great carved oak sideboard in the Tudor hall at Brows-holme in Lancashire which was made from part of the reredos, a high carved screen, from behind the high altar at Whalley Abbey, near by. It certainly has much more of an ecclesiastical than a domestic air about it.

Evidence as to what 16th-century homes were like is somewhat contradictory. The great Dutch scholar and philosopher, Erasmus, who was a friend of Henry VIII, came to England in 1518 and wrote: "The floors of the houses are strewn with clay and that covered with rushes, which are now and then renewed but not so as to disturb the foundations which sometimes remain for twenty years, nursing a collection of spittle, spilt beer, fish bones and other filth which I need not mention. From this, on any elevation of temperature, there is exhaled a vapour which in my judgment is by no means beneficial to the human constitution." What manner of furniture was used by families who seemed to have lived on a sort of very ripe compost heap?

Seventy years later a more pleasant picture of English home life was presented by William Harrison in his *Description of England*, published in 1587. Then he wrote: "The walls of our houses on the inner side in like sort be either hanged with tapestry or painted cloths or else they are ceiled [*sic.*] with oak of our own or brought hither out of the east countries. The furniture of our houses also exceedeth and herein I do not speak of the nobility and gentry only but likewise of the lowest sort in most places. Even the inferior artificers and many farmers have for the most part learned also to garnish their cupboards with plate, their joined beds with tapestry and their tables with carpets and fine napery." When first introduced, carpets served as table coverings and only began to be used as floor coverings sometime later in the 17th century.

Renaissance influence on furniture design was slow to

11

reach England. During the reign of Elizabeth I a popular form of decoration on chest panels and the backs of chairs was low relief, male or female heads carved in profile and set in round, square or triangular lozenges. This was known as *Romayne* (or Roman) *work*, clearly indicative of the country of origin.

Examples of Scottish furniture of this same period would indicate that it was developing separately but on much the same pattern as that in Elizabethan England. The influence of French and Flemish Renaissance ideas on 16th-century Scottish architecture must have affected the design of domestic woodwork as well.

By the beginning of the 17th century and the union of the English and Scottish thrones with the accession of James I in 1603, British furniture was beginning to assume more particularly national characteristics. The early Stuart period saw the introduction of upholstered *farthingale chairs*, designed for the ladies with their widespreading farthingale skirts. The heavier Tudor styles of the previous century were becoming more refined.

Charles I, son of James, was a sincere patron of the fine arts, and painters like Rubens and Van Dyck were made very welcome at the British court. Finer furniture provided the setting for the fine works which they produced. Unfortunately, this progress came to a sudden halt with the outbreak of the Civil War in 1642.

For the next eighteen years the arts, to a great extent, were dormant and contemporary writers recorded the damage done to houses and their contents by the billeted soldiery. The ten years of Commonwealth rule which followed the war was an arid period. The Puritan mind was averse to display or ornament, save of the simplest kind. The period of Cromwell's rule did, however, see the emergence of the gate-leg table, which in its various forms has remained in vogue up to the present day. Dining chairs also appeared during this Commonwealth period as rather stouter versions of the farthingale chair with a slightly lower seat and a higher back. The seat, however, was still somewhat higher than the later standard height of 18 inches. The rails between the front legs were also placed high so that heels of boots and shoes could be hooked up on them and the feet of the sitter kept well out of the draughts and cold of the stone-flagged floors. Another fashion peculiar to this period was the introduction of leather upholstery, secured with large brass dome-headed nails. Chairs finished in this way are still referred to as Cromwellian chairs.

The restoration of the monarchy in 1660 probably gave to the arts in this country the greatest impetus which they have ever sustained. It has been referred to as the beginning of the golden age of design in England. Charles II and his loyal followers had spent long years in exile, sometimes at the court of the French king, Louis XIV, and sometimes in the Netherlands. Always they had lived in a state of comparative poverty, witnesses to a life of luxury and fine living which they could envy but not emulate.

When the Cavaliers returned to their estates in England and to houses looted in the wars and scantily furnished with worn-out pieces, they made haste to set up their households again in the styles which they had got to know so well on the continent. Craftsmen hurried over the Channel to London where so much work was waiting to be done.

French chairmakers and Flemish woodcarvers brought with them foreign designs which, within a few years, were to be transformed into a truly British style. Charles II married Catherine of Braganza, a Portuguese princess, who in her train brought further continental patterns from Portugal and Spain. It was the beginning of the great age of British furniture making.

In this period of extravagant taste, baroque design reached its flamboyant peak towards the end of the 17th century. Charles II had died in 1685, his brother James II was forced to abdicate after only three years on the throne and a Dutch prince, William of Orange, was offered and accepted the British crown. William III was not only a soldier and a statesman but he was also a man with a great appreciation of the arts. He caused Hampton Court to be largely rebuilt, and much fine furniture in the Dutch style at Hampton Court today dates from this time.

The accession of William and Mary coincided with the Revocation of the Edict of Nantes. Religious persecution in France now compelled many Huguenot craftsmen to flee their country and seek a refuge in Britain. Thus, French styles were mingled with those of the Netherlands to affect the design of British furniture in the closing years of the 17th century.

Anne, last of the Stuart monarchs, succeeded William in 1702. Now was the time when restrained shaping and the natural grain of walnut unadorned were to lend a more sober charm to the furniture produced. The long Georgian period began in 1714 and for the first time history began to record some details of the lives and personalities of the great designers.

Among the most important of these was William Kent, architect and protégé of Lord Burlington. The latter had travelled widely on the continent and had developed a great love of the work of the Italian Renaissance architect, Palladio. Burlington had taken with him on his grand tour the young architect Kent, who on his return to England, was to justify fully his patron's interest by designing such notable places as Holkham Hall in Norfolk and the Horse Guards building in Whitehall.

Kent, in company with Batty Langley and other early

14

18th-century architects, was among the first to design not only a house but also its contents. It followed that their designs had an architectural bias and such features as the broken pediment and applied pilaster were typical, and although Kent's furniture was often heavy and elaborate it had the very spirit of early Georgian fashion.

Towards the middle of the 18th century, taste was changing in favour of the lighter and more gracious rococo style. Born amid the luxury of the French court it manifested itself in England as a liking for Chinese, asymmetrical shapes and a revived Gothic, in romantic form. Claydon House in Buckinghamshire and Horace Walpole's Strawberry Hill, built over the years from 1753 to 1776, are very fine examples of this time.

Some men more than others, who may have been of equal talent, are remembered as being typical of their age. Such was the great cabinet-maker and designer, Thomas Chippendale. He has been accused of plagiarising the designs of others but he is best remembered for his *Gentleman and Cabinet-maker's Director*, published in 1754. This was a beautifully produced book of furniture designs showing the sort of things which might be had from the Chippendale workshops. It might even be referred to as an 18th-century mail order catalogue. There is no doubt that Chippendale in his own time was accepted as a man of outstanding talent, as a friend of Sir Joshua Reynolds and as a member of the Society of Arts.

Another 18th-century architect whose name is especially associated with fine furniture was Robert Adam. He loved the "beautiful spirit of antiquity" and, like William Kent before him, went to the ancient Greek and Roman patterns for his inspiration. Adam employed both Chippendale and Hepplewhite to carry out his furniture designs. Chippendale he disliked, perhaps because a certain intellectual pride could not tolerate another way

15

of thinking or a mind so different from his own. Hepple-white, on the other hand, could be relied upon to carry out his designs to the letter and Adam was very apprecia-tive of the work of "honest George". Some of Adam's best work was done at Syon House.

Hepplewhite is probably best remembered for his chair backs and for the tapering, fluted legs on his tables. He also produced a book of designs, the *Cabinet-maker and Upholsterer's Guide*, but he had been dead two years when the first edition appeared in 1788.

It is important, at this stage, to appreciate that when speaking of Chippendale or Hepplewhite furniture, or that of any other well-known designer, it is not implied that the furniture in question was actually made by the craftsman whose name is used to describe it. Only in a few instances, where receipted bills are in existence as at Harewood House in Yorkshire, can it be proved that the pieces were made in the workshop of a particular craftsman or designer. In this case the accounts of the time show that Thomas Chippendale made certain sets of chairs and tables to the design of Robert Adam.

The name of any particular designer used to describe a piece of furniture merely denotes the period during which many cabinet-makers were completing work in the current styles of that time. There were a considerable number of craftsmen in the mid-18th century, like Ince and Mayhew or Vile and Cobb, whose work is held to be equal to if not superior to that of the more well-known makers.

It must also be appreciated that periods overlapped considerably and that styles which were fashionable in London, Edinburgh and Dublin, would not penetrate to the provincial towns until some considerable time later. Thus furniture, in the Queen Anne pattern, though ousted by the designs of Kent or Langley, would still be made in the remoter areas some twenty years later. Ideas were slow to travel in the 18th century but much country-made furniture has considerable charm.

The 18th century closed with the enigmatic figure of Thomas Sheraton, secure for all time among the number of the great furniture designers. Sheraton had had some training as a cabinet-maker in his youth but preferred to think of himself as a teacher of drawing and a non-conformist preacher. Whatever his ambitions were, his personal life was a failure by normal standards and he died when comparatively young in poverty and obscurity. Although it is doubtful if he ever actually made a piece of furniture his clean cut, slender and often very ingenious designs gave to the cabinet-makers of his day a wonderful source of inspiration with the publication of his two works, the *Cabinet-maker's and Upholsterer's Drawing Book* and his *Cabinet Dictionary* of 1803.

Although the early years of the 19th century found England locked in the struggle of the Napoleonic wars it was a time of changing fashions still. Strangely enough the basic ideas seem to have been borrowed from the enemy, and French Empire designs, influenced by conquests in Italy and Egypt, are to be found in much of the Regency furniture made between 1810 and 1830.

Now began the long decline to the later Victorian period, but the Georgian love of fine things was to influence the design of much attractive furniture still to be made.

The rosewood and walnut furniture of the early Victorians reflected both a second Gothic revival and the romantic mood evoked by Sir Walter Scott's Abbotsford novels. Many fine pieces of delicate, if rather fussy, design were made, faintly echoing the greatness which had gone before.

GOTHIC STOOL SHOWING
ARCHITECTURAL INFLUENCE
C. 1450

TUDOR CHEST WITH
ROMAYNE CARVING
C. 1550

EARLY STUART
FARTHINGALE CHAIR
C. 1620

COMMONWEALTH
GATELEG TABLE
C. 1650

RESTORATION CHAIR
C. 1670

WILLIAM AND MARY
BAROQUE STOOL
C. 1690

QUEEN ANNE
WRITING TABLE
C. 1710

WILLIAM KENT
BOOKCASE C. 1730

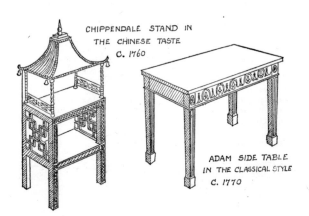

CHIPPENDALE STAND IN
THE CHINESE TASTE
C. 1760

ADAM SIDE TABLE
IN THE CLASSICAL STYLE
C. 1770

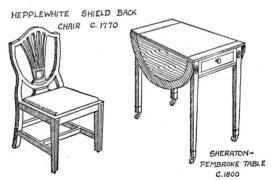

HEPPLEWHITE SHIELD BACK
CHAIR C. 1770

SHERATON-
PEMBROKE TABLE
C. 1800

CHAPTER 2

Materials and Processes

The Age of Oak—early painted woodwork—the period of the
oiner—pinned mortise and tenon joints—Tudor carving and early
tuart turning—inlaid decoration—bobbin and baluster legs—
introduction of upholstery—the Restoration and the Age of Walnut—
the joiner becomes a cabinet-maker—the new techniques—dovetailing and spiral twists—veneering, parquetry and marquetry—
split cane seating—cabinet feet and leg stretchers—introduction of
lacquering and japanning—17th and 18th century "Do-it-yourself"
—the Age of Mahogany—Satinwood and painted furniture—
Regency Rosewood and the return of Walnut—papier mâché and
mother of pearl—nails and screws—handles, locks and metal ornament—wood finishes.

Domestic woodwork, until the Restoration of 1660, was
almost invariably carried out in oak. This typically
British wood was so hard, tough and difficult to work
that this was probably one of the chief factors in producing
the solid, angular appearance of early furniture.

Traces of polychrome paintwork, in the corners and
cracks of some furniture surviving from the Gothic
period indicate that the better examples of that time were
probably painted all over in brilliant colours of red, blue
and gold. Although the rooms were sparsely furnished,
the effect of these brightly coloured pieces must have done
much to relieve the gloom of the living quarters.

In early times, and as indicated by the passage quoted
in Chapter 1 from Wm. Harrison's account, considerable
quantities of oak were imported from Germany and the
Baltic states. This was known as *wagenschot* oak and was
straight grained, well figured and much easier to work than

the British variety. Moreover, British oak was always much in demand for shipbuilding and for the frame constructions of the Tudor half-timbered houses. So scarce did British oak become by the second half of the 17th century that an embargo had to be placed on the use of oak for anything but shipbuilding.

The word *wagenschot* in time became absorbed into the English language as wainscot and as such it is known; usually it is applied to wall panelling, but many old inventories refer to wainscot chests and tables.

All early furniture was assembled by nailing or was pegged together with wooden pegs. This method was referred to as carpenters' work. By the end of the Middle Ages much fine, if somewhat sturdy woodwork was being skilfully put together with joints like the mortise and tenon and trench joint. The use and development of the mortise and tenon, known in Egyptian and Roman times, enabled much lighter furniture to be made by using panelled instead of solid bodywork.

The architectural nature of much Gothic woodwork is further indicated by the form of mitre joint used in the construction of panelling.

Here the joiner was faithfully imitating a mason's construction for a mitre, a method which the mason was forced to adopt because of the nature of the material in which he was working. When the joiner discovered that the grain of wood permitted a simpler and neater joint, then the mason's mitre was discarded.

No glue was used by the early joiners but the mortise and tenons were held together with oak pegs. These were dried in an oven and when driven into the hole prepared in the joint, the normal damp in the atmosphere would cause the peg to swell and so lock it in position. The proximity of the peghole to the shoulder of the tenon prevented the wood splitting. The carpenters and joiners belonged to separate trade guilds and demarcation of work was jealously safeguarded even in those far off days.

One of the earliest decorative motifs carved in wood was the trailing vine and although Gothic in origin its use persisted until late in the 17th century. Early versions of this design were deeply carved and this method was typical of much early work. Romayne work and heavy bulbous turnings, adorned with acanthus leaves, on beds, tables and presses were characteristic of mid-16th-century work. Towards the end of Elizabeth's reign, however, the carving had become less free and tended more to low relief and repeated strapwork patterns.

Another form of decoration about this time was the use of inlaid, multi-coloured woods of local origin. Those used were bog-oak, to simulate ebony, yellow box and white holly. Sometimes the holly was stained with green dye but this usually faded. The different woods were inlaid in panels in the form of geometrical designs or conventional floral patterns. These latter should not be confused with the floral marquetry decoration on furniture, so popular about one hundred years later.

Early Stuart woodwork of the reigns of James I and Charles I shows the use made of turning for ornament and decoration. Legs of baluster shape were used on stools, chairs and tables and split turnings and small pilasters were applied to uprights, rails and panels. Simple mouldings, mitred and applied in geometric patterns were also used by the middle of the century in conjunction with applied split turnings.

Upholstery for chairs and stools was an innovation during the early years of James's reign. Springing, of course, was not introduced until Victorian times but well-padded seats and backs of chairs were covered with tapestry. In fact, the idea of covering woodwork with material was extended to the overall coverage of legs as well as arms and seats with brass nail studded velvet. This fashion was, however, short lived and the practice died out with the Civil War. Squab chairs with wooden seats covered with tied-on cushions known as *squabs* continued in use throughout the 17th century.

The Restoration of the monarchy in 1660, bringing with it so many new ideas, saw the emergence of a more highly skilled craftsman than the joiner. He became known as a cabinet-maker and with him a whole new series of techniques for the construction and ornamentation of furniture developed.

The cabinet-maker began by improving the method of making dovetail joints so that the drawers for his new cabinets could be made more neatly yet stronger than before. The broad surfaces produced in the new methods of cabinet construction lent themselves to ornamentation by veneering. This practice is often a matter for misunderstanding by many who look upon veneering as a sham to cover inferior workmanship. This might be so in the 20th century, as far as some cheap furniture is concerned, but veneering in the 17th and 18th centuries was practised solely because it was the best method of displaying the lovely and colourful grain of burr walnut. Certain of the rarer and more expensive woods like laburnum, kingwood and ebony could only be obtained in very narrow boards and were far too heavy and dense in texture to be used in the solid.

The more experienced craftsmen always chose pine for the carcass or bodywork of the piece to be veneered. This was because pine, when well seasoned, was very stable and did not shrink, swell or twist with changes in the atmosphere. Oak, on the other hand, will move many years after it might be presumed to be thoroughly seasoned and it does not make a good base for a veneer for that reason. The better cabinet-made drawers, for example, would have a pine front to take the veneer and oak linings to stand up to wear. The doors of long case clocks with walnut veneered on oak are often found with the veneer split across where the top batten of the door has shrunk.

A more advanced form of veneering was practised with the use of parquetry and marquetry. The processes in both cases were very similar. Sheets of different coloured veneers were held together with a paper pattern on the top. The design was cut out as in fretwork with the aid of a marquetry-cutter's donkey, which was a sort of heavy fretsawing device. The resulting jigsaws of coloured shapes were then fitted together and glued on a sheet of paper, resulting in as many panels as there had been sheets of veneer to begin with. The process was Dutch in origin but it is generally accepted that it was brought to perfection by the British cabinet-makers.

Designs which were geometrical in form are known as parquetry and were usually set in a ground of oystershell veneer cut on the cross from small laburnum logs. Marquetry was more free and usually representational and dated from around 1680. At first the designs, composed of birds and flowers, were laid out in small panels but later all-over marquetry became the fashion. The effect was rather over-decorative and a third stage was more subdued. This was called *seaweed* marquetry and the all-over pattern was executed in closely interwoven arabesques. Marquetry went out of fashion towards the end of the reign of William III but was re-introduced by Robert Adam about 1770. In the form of classical arrangements of musical instruments and flowers it was used to ornament the tops and fronts of satinwood tables and commodes.

Veneered surfaces were usually surrounded by a border of veneer known as *cross-banding*, when a wood similar to the main veneer or one contrasting in grain and colour was used. On the plainer country pieces, where the craftsman had not mastered the art of over-all veneering or where economy of the rarer woods was essential, it became the custom to inlay a border of cross-banding around the edge of a table, chest top or a drawer front.

During the first half of the 18th century much country furniture in oak was cross-banded with walnut or pollard oak. This latter wood, similar in grain to burr walnut, was obtained from the stumps of cut-down oak trees which had been allowed to grow again. Later, mahogany was used and although not so effective in appearance, it became very popular in the provinces. Most of this mahogany cross-banded furniture seems to have originated in Lancashire and Cheshire.

Marquetry in ormolu and tortoiseshell appeared on some French furniture imported into this country during the second half of the 18th century. This form of ornamentation had been devised by Charles André Boulle, cabinet-maker to Louis XIV, but it never became very popular and very little was made in Britain.

Some early Queen Anne cabinets, veneered in walnut, have been found with lines of pewter set in the veneer but inlaid metal did not become generally fashionable until the Regency.

Another important feature of the Restoration period was the adoption of walnut as cabinet-making material. There were many reasons for the popularity of walnut, chief among which were that it was a close-grained hardwood of an attractive colour and more capable of being shaped and carved than the more intractable oak. It has been stated that walnut trees planted at the end of Elizabeth's reign had, in seventy years, grown to a stage where they could be usefully converted into timber for woodworking. Antique British walnut has that unmistakable, honey-coloured glow about it which is so attractive, but quite large quantities of French and the darker Italian walnut were imported, so great was the demand.

Oak continued to be used by the joiners, working in the provinces and still using the traditional methods, but their work always bore the stamp of the homely artisan rather than that of the artist craftsman. Fashionable furniture, whatever the period and whether the material was walnut, mahogany or satinwood, was copied by the country woodworkers in oak or fruitwood. From early times, much domestic woodwork was made in local woods such as apple, pear, cherry and yew and sometimes there would be a mixture of woods in one article.

The reason why so many of these earlier mixed wood pieces have failed to survive is that they were all very susceptible to attack by woodworm. Walnut wood was particularly vulnerable in this respect and it is due to this cause that walnut furniture of the late 17th and early 18th centuries is so scarce and expensive.

A particular feature of Restoration walnut work was the spiral or *barley-sugar twist* for chair backs and the legs of tables. It was a design which emanated from Spain early in the 17th century, was adopted by the French and from there carried over to England. Although turning continued in popularity throughout the 17th century, the sliding tool rest for a lathe had not yet been introduced and all spiral twists had to be finished by hand. This and so much else of the excellent craftsmanship of the period show what a high degree of skill the late 17th-century craftsman had reached.

Split cane seating for chairs and day-beds was an attempt to provide rather more resilience than had been possible with previous attempts at upholstery. Long lengths of thinly split cane were woven across the seat rails in a honeycomb pattern, producing a springy support for an overlay cushion but the method became obsolete when improved ideas in upholstery were introduced in Queen Anne's reign.

Some features of the William and Mary period were the

turned bun feet, applied to desks, chests of drawers, cabinets and even long case clocks. Turned chair and table legs had the shape known as *ball and cup* while the hitherto straight stretchers used to strengthen legs were now placed diagonally in an attractively curved form.

The growing trade of the East India Company brought many prized commodities to Britain's shores like porcelain, spices and tea. These were often packed in lacquered chests which proved so attractive that cupboards lacquered in black, blue, red, green and yellow with raised gilded designs on them were also ordered from the eastern merchants. Some authorities consider that imitation lacquer cabinets made in this country often had the doors sent to the East to be lacquered by the native craftsmen.

This vogue for lacquered cabinets caused a method to be developed at home for producing a similar effect with paint and varnish, known as japanning. Although not nearly so durable or effective as lacquer the process had the advantage that it could be carried out by amateurs. The modern enthusiasm for home handicrafts is by no means a new thing, and it is not generally realised that in the late 17th and throughout the 18th centuries there was a considerable vogue among the leisured classes for "Do-it-yourself" activities. A "Know How" book was published in 1688 by John Stalker and George Parker, which was called *A Treatise of Japanning and Varnishing*. It had a considerable success at the time and was recently reprinted in a facsimile edition.

Mention must be made here of the *cabriole leg*, used on chairs and tables during the first half of the 18th century. It evolved from the scrolled foot of the baroque William and Mary era and reached its purest and most attractive form during the reign of Queen Anne.

The steady growth of trade with the West Indies and the Spanish possessions in Central and South America introduced a new wood, mahogany, for the cabinet-maker's use. It did not come immediately into favour, although Kent and some other designers used it occasionally for their furniture. A prohibitive import duty almost put an end to its employment in this country but when this tax was repealed in 1733, mahogany soon became the fashionable wood of the times.

Circumstances favoured the beginnings of the Age of Mahogany. In the first place, a shortage of French walnut had occurred, due to a virulent disease among the trees in France. Furthermore, it was discovered that mahogany was not only pleasing to the eye with its rich colour and grain but also it was a very strong and workable timber. Most important factor in its favour was an almost complete immunity to attack by woodworm. Mahogany, then, had everything to recommend it and its popularity as a furnishing wood has never waned.

The first shipments of mahogany came from Cuba and this was a dark coloured timber with a close, well-figured grain. Later in the century, as supplies from Cuba became exhausted a variety, lighter in weight and known as Honduras mahogany or baywood from the Central American mainland, began to replace it. The colour of the Honduras wood was lighter than the Cuban variety and it came from a bigger tree. Consequently, it was available in very wide boards which were admirably suited for the long, Georgian multi-leaved dining tables. Cuban mahogany was initially used as a solid material but when cut into veneers it was discovered that the effect was very much more decorative.

Mahogany was essentially a Georgian wood and while the names of Chippendale and Hepplewhite are traditionally coupled with it, another wood is usually associated with the names of Adam and Sheraton. This was satinwood, a light yellow coloured timber with a smooth grain like shot silk. It was particularly suited to the finer and more delicate designs which were fashionable towards the end of the 18th century. It made a becoming background to the painted flower swags and small illuminated panels which artists like Angelica Kauffmann would paint on them. Adam also used beech for his chairs which were all-over painted in black or white with gilded lines. Again, the woodworm has rendered this beech furniture comparatively rare.

Rosewood was the next timber which took pride of place in the Regency and early Victorian eras. It is a dark brown, striped wood, closely related to and very similar in appearance to the kingwood of the 17th century. Being rather heavy, rosewood was often used as a veneer on pine, and inlaid brass frets and stringing were characteristic of the Regency period.

Walnut returned to favour in the mid-19th century and with it, for a short time, black japanned papier mâché, which was inlaid with mother of pearl and painted with flowers. This last medium was used for a whole variety of objects such as light boudoir chairs, sewing tables, clock cases and light furniture generally. It did not remain in vogue for very long.

For joining wood together, nails had been in use from very early times and a hand-wrought, broad-headed pattern, known as a *clout nail*, was employed until the middle of the 18th century when a simpler shaped, hand-cut nail was adopted. Screws appeared in the second half of the 17th century but hinges and locks were very often secured with clout nails on country-made oak desks and cupboards until the beginning of the Georgian period. Early screws had a longer threaded portion and very short shanks and were made without points until around 1850.

Metal hinges for small doors and box lids during the

16th and 17th centuries were made of wrought iron and were usually of a butterfly or cock's-head shape. With the advent of the cabinet-maker, smaller brass hinges of plain rectangular shape were developed and these were fitted so that only the knuckle of the hinge showed. The cock's-head pattern was later modified to a simpler "H" shape and this was used on corner cupboards almost until the end of the 18th century.

Keyholes in 17th-century drawers and cupboards were protected against key wear by fitting *escutcheon*, or *scutcheon*, *plates* over the keyholes. As from the introduction of mahogany these were replaced by inset brass keyhole rims which have continued in use up to the present day. Bone and mother of pearl escutcheon plates, inset around the keyhole, are to be found in furniture dating from about 1790 to 1840. When there is doubt over the age of small locks, it should be remembered that keys prior to the Victorian period had the wards filed on the front edge and not along the bottom in order to fit the earlier style of lock.

Cast metal ornaments made of ormolu, a form of gilded brass, were introduced from France about 1750. These were applied as ornaments to mahogany and satinwood tables and cabinets designed in the later rococo style. The British products in ormolu were an improvement on the French versions by more skilful chiselling and chasing before they were gilded.

Except for the polychrome furniture of the early Gothic period, domestic woodwork was usually left in its natural state, apart from being polished with linseed oil and beeswax. What is not generally appreciated is that the Elizabethans did not live in an atmosphere of dark brown oak furniture. Their woodwork was of a light straw colour which has only become dark with time. In the 17th century varnish was used on oak while the finer walnut veneered furniture was carefully polished with walnut oil and wax before leaving the workshop.

The popularity of mahogany during the Georgian period led to the treating of oak and fruitwood with a coat of varnish mixed with ox-blood to produce the appearance of mahogany. The author once purchased a long case clock for £10 in a sale room. It had a slim case with a little brass-framed, bull's-eye window in the door and all the appearance of a clock of about 1700. The wood, however, was of a red mahogany colour and only a closer examination revealed, beneath the varnish, cross-banded and burr walnut veneer. The little window in the door gave the first clue, because this feature in long case clocks had become obsolete before mahogany came into general use.

Fortunately, the well waxed walnut had prevented the penetration of the ox-blood varnish into the grain and this was painstakingly removed to reveal a lovely, honey coloured burr walnut case. The urge felt by some Georgian to "keep up with the Joneses" by modernising a walnut clock, out-of-fashion in the mid-18th century, had provided, two hundred years later, a clock for the author for £10. When completely restored this clock was of a value around the £100 mark.

French polishing was introduced into the British Isles about 1820 and many fine old pieces of furniture were deprived of the lovely patina which only years of constant polishing with wax could produce. They were then given the hard, glassy, easily marked surface by the French-polisher, which fails completely to accord with the antique appearance of the past.

JOINTS AND ORNAMENTS

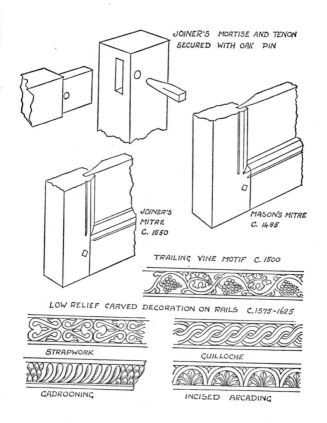

JOINER'S MORTISE AND TENON
SECURED WITH OAK PIN

JOINER'S
MITRE
C. 1550

MASON'S MITRE
C. 1485

TRAILING VINE MOTIF C. 1500

LOW RELIEF CARVED DECORATION ON RAILS C. 1575-1625

STRAPWORK

GUILLOCHE

GADROONING

INCISED ARCADING

FLORAL AND GEOMETRICAL
PATTERNS INLAID WITH BOX
AND BOG OAK C. 1610

BRITISH C. 1580

BULBOUS
TURNED
LEGS

BRITISH C. 1620

DUTCH C. 1620

RAIL INLAID
WITH BOX AND
BOG OAK C. 1620

ARCADED
CARVED
PANEL C. 1620

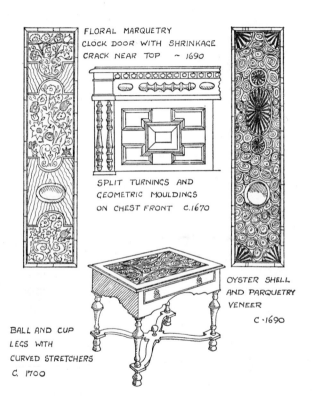

FLORAL MARQUETRY
CLOCK DOOR WITH SHRINKAGE
CRACK NEAR TOP ~ 1690

SPLIT TURNINGS AND
GEOMETRIC MOULDINGS
ON CHEST FRONT C.1670

OYSTER SHELL
AND PARQUETRY
VENEER
C ·1690

BALL AND CUP
LEGS WITH
CURVED STRETCHERS
C. 1700

NAILS, SCREWS AND FITTINGS

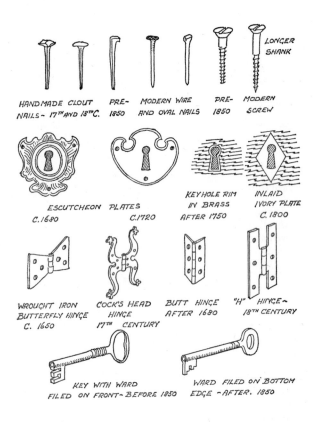

LONGER SHANK

HANDMADE CLOUT NAILS~ 17ᵀᴴ AND 18ᵀᴴ C.

PRE-1850

MODERN WIRE AND OVAL NAILS

PRE-1850

MODERN SCREW

ESCUTCHEON PLATES
C. 1680   C. 1720

KEYHOLE RIM IN BRASS AFTER 1750

INLAID IVORY PLATE C. 1800

WROUGHT IRON BUTTERFLY HINGE C. 1650

COCK'S HEAD HINGE 17ᵀᴴ CENTURY

BUTT HINGE AFTER 1680

"H" HINGE~ 18ᵀᴴ CENTURY

KEY WITH WARD FILED ON FRONT~ BEFORE 1850

WARD FILED ON BOTTOM EDGE ~AFTER. 1850

36

CHAPTER 3

Chests, Chests of Drawers and Various Small Boxes

Origins of the chest—cofferers and arkwrights—the carpenter's planked chest—chip-carving decoration—the panelled chest of the joiner—development of the mule chest—early enclosed chest of drawers—the chest in two stages—the joiner's slide—veneered chests—chests on stands and tallboys—bachelor, dressing and linen chests with presses—commodes and military chests—later forms—drawer construction and dating by feet and handles—Bible and ruff boxes—knife and candle boxes—tea caddies, cellarets and portable liqueur cases—sewing boxes.

Chests belong to the very beginning of domestic furnishing. Blanket chests, hope chests, even treasure chests—they served as wardrobes, as safes, as seats and sometimes even as beds. A chest is probably one of the earliest pieces likely to come the way of anyone starting to collect antique furniture in a modest manner. Those belonging to the early Stuart period are not difficult to find and may be had for under £10. They are not always large and a length of 3 feet or very little more is fairly common.

Very early chests, some of which may date from Saxon times, were primitive but served their purpose well. Usually they were made from rough hewn logs which were sawn down the middle and hollowed out. Then the two parts were hinged together and encircled with strong iron bands to which locks could be attached. The French word *tronc*, meaning a collecting box, and the English trunk have the same origin and refer to this tree-bole type of chest. I have seen one in the church at Llan Eilean, near Amlwch in Anglesey, with three locks. It was customary

37

for the keys to be held by the priest and two churchwardens so that the chest could not be opened without all three being present.

Medieval chests for transporting money and valuables were known as coffers. They were comparatively small and often covered with leather and studded with nails. The man who made them was known as a cofferer and another craftsman who made chests was called an arkwright. He made them with bevelled lids and wooden pins served as hinges. These belong to the Gothic period and are very rare.

The early Tudor chests, made for the smaller household, were known as planked chests. They were made by a carpenter and consisted of a number of boards or planks held together with nails or wooden pins. Planked chests had thick iron wire or wrought-iron strap hinges and were often decorated with chip-carving or architectural motifs in low relief. Some of these planked chests were quite small and make interesting acquisitions for those who like old oak.

The joiner's panelled chest appeared about 1550 and the panels were usually decorated like the example shown in Chapter 1. The panelled chest, in various sizes, was an essential chattel in every Tudor household and the larger establishments seem to have had a chest in every room. Visitors to Haddon Hall in Derbyshire may care to count the great number and variety of chests which are to be seen there. A type of chest, made about this time, which is now very rare and really a collector's piece, was one constructed with fairly long legs, about table height. It was known as a *counter* and used by house stewards and clerks for paying out or collecting money. The modern word counter, as in a shop, derives from this long obsolete piece of furniture. In a slightly different form, with doors opening at the front and with the top fastened down, the counter was known as a *hutch*. Further details of this are given in Chapter 6.

The ordinary planked or panelled chest had one great drawback in that only the contents at the top were readily accessible. To reach anything carefully tucked away at the bottom of the chest necessitated the removal of all the other things lying above. Early in the Stuart period, some ingenious joiner invented the *mule chest*. This was a shallower type of panelled chest, under which were situated two or three drawers. This design was extremely popular and mule chests continued to be made in the country towns and villages until around the year 1800.

The mule chest proved to be a great improvement in its capacity for storage. Not only were the bottom drawers available for the separation of items, but inside the chest itself it is not unusual to find a small box or till with a lid, situated at one end near the top. This was used for keeping letters and documents and these little tills often repay a closer examination, for on several occasions I have found that the front of the box will slide upwards to reveal two or three secret drawers beneath. In some of the larger chests, intended for storing blankets or linen only, the till would be merely a shallow tray on which the good housewife could place a spray of lavender to sweeten her sheets and pillow slips.

To the student of woodwork history, the mule chest is particularly interesting because there can be little doubt that the chest of drawers developed from it. This process was not a swift one and for a space of time, roughly between 1620 and 1660, there was a type of chest of drawers in use which was really a cupboard full of trays or drawers, surmounted by one large deep drawer. The cupboard doors with one lock prevented unauthorised access to any of the lower drawers but this must have proved unworkable as this pattern ceased to be made shortly after 1660 and the chest of drawers assumed the form by which it is known today.

For ease of removal the first chests of drawers were made in two stages or sections. The upper stage of two small and one long drawer fitted on to four pegs on top of the lower section of two long drawers. These early chests in two stages also had drawers with grooves cut in the sides, known as *joiner's slides*. They were designed mainly to prevent wear on the drawer bottoms and also to prevent the drawer from tipping downwards when more than half open. It was found, however, that the slide grooves required disproportionately thicker linings to the drawers so that the cabinet-maker, with his improved ideas of jointing and finer standard of craftsmanship, caused the joiner's slide to become obsolete about the year 1690. Any antique chest of drawers with joiner's slides may be safely said to be earlier than this date although this ancient construction has been revived in the last few years for modern kitchen units and office furniture.

Cabinet-maker's chests with their broad, flat surfaces provided suitable subjects for veneering. By the end of the Restoration period, chests with marquetry decoration were in fashion and it is not uncommon to find country-made oak chests of this time with panelled oak sides and the top and drawer fronts veneered. Smaller chests of drawers, of 3-feet width and under and covered with oystershell veneer, are scarce and in good condition might be worth up to £80 and more.

During the William and Mary period, the chest of drawers on a stand made its appearance and shortly after developed into a chest on a chest or tallboy. The chest on a stand did not last long as a furnishing piece but the tallboy remained popular throughout the greater part of the 18th century. It is difficult to understand this, as access to the upper drawers of a tallboy is very awkward and necessitates standing on a chair or stool. Perhaps, for this very reason, they were considered safer for the storage of valuables.

Bachelor chests and dressing chests were brought into use during the first half of the 18th century. These were intended primarily for bedrooms, the former having a folding top which opened outwards on *lopers*, or pull-out supports. Sometimes, instead of the folding top, a pull-out slide for brushing clothes was included in the construction. The dressing chest had a top drawer fitted with a toilet set and further reference will be made to it in Chapter 9.

Another type, adapted for a special purpose, was the linen chest with a press. It was usually about 3 feet long and had several small drawers near the top. Its particular feature was a wooden screw-press, mounted on the top for the purpose of compressing the linen before putting it away in the drawers. On several occasions I have come across these chests, with rectangular pieces of wood let into the top at each end to fill the spaces left where the screw-press uprights had been removed.

Two other varieties belong to the Chippendale and Sheraton periods. One was the commode, a very elaborate chest of drawers which was raised on shaped legs. It often had a convex or *bombé* front and later types were embellished with ormolu mounts in the French style. The other was the military chest, used during the campaigns of the Napoleonic wars in the early 19th century. It was made in two stages for ease of transport and is easily recognised by the clean-cut rectangular shape, the addition of brass corner pieces and the sunk handles on the drawers. A design usually associated with Sheraton was the bow-fronted chest and these continued to be made well into Victorian times.

Certain details of drawer construction, handle design

and feet are invaluable in dating a chest of drawers. Dovetailing of a rather crude nature had been used for the corners of boxes and small chests before the Restoration. During the years between 1660 and 1750 the technique of making fine dovetail joints was brought to a high degree of craftsmanship. Large tails and widely spaced pins are indicative of early or country production. Herring-bone stringing, set in walnut veneer, was used for drawer front decoration during the Queen Anne period but became obsolete soon after 1720.

Oak chests of drawers, belonging to the second half of the 17th century and the early years of the 18th, are sometimes found with the corner joints lapped and nailed. This is, of course, the mark of a poorly made piece. I believe the idea of nailing drawer fronts was adapted from cheap, imported furniture and the practice was undoubtedly followed by our own country joiners, of whom a few were prepared to produce shoddy furniture, even in those days.

Until the time of Hepplewhite, drawer bottoms consisted of thin boards, fitted into a rebate on the inside of the drawer front and nailed along the under edge of the back lining. About 1775, a new method of securing the bottom appeared whereby a centre batten running from the front to the back of the drawer held the bottom boards in grooves whilst the boards, instead of being placed from front to back, now ran parallel to the drawer front.

Bun feet were the normal means of support for chests until around 1700 when bracket feet were introduced. At first, bracket feet were high and appeared out of proportion but by 1750 they were made lower and continued so until the end of the century. Cabinet-makers during the Chippendale era used bracket feet of an ogee shape on the better class of work, but these lent a heavy, baroque appearance to the chest. A lighter type of foot, known as the French foot and associated with Sheraton furniture, is usually found on the earlier bow-fronted chests. After the Regency, this design was displaced by an uglier, turned foot which remained in use until the mid-Victorian period.

The first chests of drawers had brass, drop handles which were pear shaped or flat with split ends. These handles were fixed to the drawer by means of a split pin, which passed through the drawer front and was then opened out on the inside and the ends driven into the wood. Small wooden knobs were also in use at this time but these became obsolete and did not reappear until they were adopted by Hepplewhite for his mahogany chests about 1775. Drop handles were succeeded by a ring type around 1700 and these are sometimes referred to as *Dutch drops*. From these developed loop handles with brass back plates which were first seen from about 1710. To begin with, back plates were simple butterfly shapes but by 1730 had become very elaborate, in a variety of fretted and saw-pierced patterns. By 1750, the back plates to drawer handles had disappeared, being replaced by small circular discs behind the handle mounts. Towards the end of the century knobs of cast brass or wood superseded the loop type of handle and were in use well into the Victorian period. Back plates, either round or octagonal in shape and with longer loop handles attached, were revived during the time of the Regency.

Among the more diminutive chests and boxes which were made during the 17th century was one type, about 20 inches long and 14 inches wide. It was used for storing the large, black letter family Bible or for documents. Another box, not quite so long and narrower, was used for keeping lace and neck-ruffs. It was really an early form of collar box. These boxes were usually made in oak with hasp locks and were decorated with chip-carving and gouge-cuts. These small chests should not be confused with the sloping topped table desk which will be dealt with in the chapter on desks and bureaux.

Candle and salt boxes were in everyday use in the kitchens during the 17th and 18th centuries, those for candles being long and comparatively narrow to accommodate tapers as well as candles. Later examples were often made in oak with mahogany cross-banded edges.

Table knives, particularly those with silver handles, were carefully safeguarded in the dining room. In the Chippendale period, beautifully veneered and inlaid knife-boxes were made to stand on the sideboard, while similar boxes were provided for spoons and forks. Servants of the 18th century must have been notoriously dishonest or masters and mistresses of an equally suspicious nature, for it was the practice never to allow the cutlery and silver to be removed from the dining room. After a meal the knives, forks and spoons would be washed at the sideboard and the butler would then count and lock them away in their respective boxes.

Tea was an expensive commodity between 1700 and 1800 and here again a special little box or coffer, which could be kept locked, was used to hold the precious leaves. Tea was always made at the tea table and the mistress of the house would keep the key of the tea caddy among the other housewifely belongings which hung on the chatelaine from her waist.

Tea caddies usually had two compartments, lined with lead foil to preserve the tea, but those dating from the early years of the 19th century are sometimes found with a cut-glass sugar bowl of Irish glass, situated between the compartments. A collection of wooden tea caddies is an admirable way of getting together, in a small space, examples of all the different types of wood and the decorative processes used by the cabinet-makers of the 18th century.

Reference must be made to the wine cellarets and

portable liqueur cases, which were in general use between 1775 and 1830. The cellaret was a heavy, strongly made coffer about 2 feet square and lined with lead. It stood on feet and was placed beneath a side-table in the dining room. Cellarets were nearly always made of mahogany with large brass ring handles at the sides.

The portable liqueur case was essentially a travelling companion and contained four or six square shaped decanters whose contents would fortify the traveller on the long coach journeys of those days. It was often finely veneered in walnut or mahogany and strengthened, like the military chest, with engraved brass corner pieces. These, in the finer examples, were sometimes of chased silver. I have seen these little chests made in oak, shaped like a trunk and reinforced with wrought-iron bands. As these oak types usually contain Liège glass decanters I think they must be of French or Flemish origin.

Ladies' sewing and needlework boxes, particularly those of the first half of the 19th century, can still be purchased for a pound or two. They are usually veneered in walnut or mahogany with ebony or brass inlay or with rosewood inlaid with ivory. A popular form of decoration at this time consisted of a very fine parquetry in various coloured woods, known as Tunbridge ware. These work boxes can be included, to advantage, with a collection of tea caddies and other small boxes.

EARLY CHESTS

PLANKED CHEST
WITH CHIP-CARVING
C. 1485

COUNTER OR
CHEST ON LEGS
C. 1550

MULE CHEST WITH
TWO DRAWERS UNDER
C. 1620

JOINED CHEST OF
DRAWERS IN TWO STAGES
C. 1650

17TH AND 18TH-CENTURY CHESTS

CHEST OF DRAWERS C. 1670
SHOWING STAGES SEPARATED
AND JOINERS SLIDE IN TOP DRAWER

CHEST OF DRAWERS
ON STAND C. 1710

HERRING BONE STRINGING

CHEST ON A CHEST
OR TALLBOY C. 1725

BACHELOR'S CHEST
WITH OGEE FEET,
CANTED CORNERS AND
BRUSHING SLIDE C. 1760

CHESTS OF DRAWERS

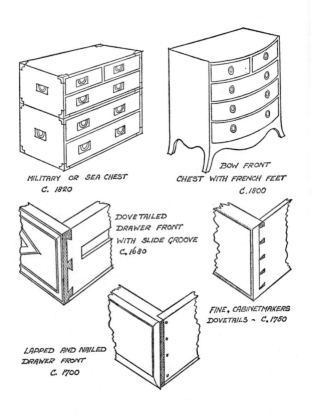

MILITARY OR SEA CHEST
C. 1820

BOW FRONT
CHEST WITH FRENCH FEET
C. 1800

DOVETAILED
DRAWER FRONT
WITH SLIDE GROOVE
C. 1680

FINE, CABINETMAKERS
DOVETAILS ~ C. 1750

LAPPED AND NAILED
DRAWER FRONT
C. 1700

DETAILS OF CHESTS OF DRAWERS

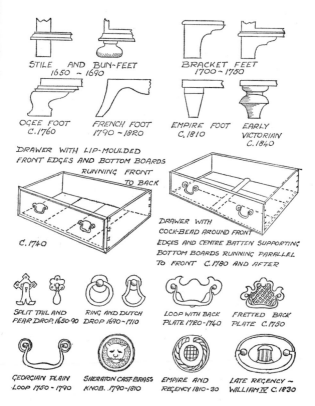

STILE AND BUN-FEET
1650 ~ 1690

BRACKET FEET
1700 ~ 1750

OGEE FOOT
C. 1760

FRENCH FOOT
1790 ~ 1820

EMPIRE FOOT
C. 1810

EARLY VICTORIAN
C. 1840

DRAWER WITH LIP-MOULDED FRONT EDGES AND BOTTOM BOARDS RUNNING FRONT TO BACK

C. 1740

DRAWER WITH COCK-BEAD AROUND FRONT EDGES AND CENTRE BATTEN SUPPORTING BOTTOM BOARDS RUNNING PARALLEL TO FRONT C. 1780 AND AFTER

SPLIT TAIL AND PEAR DROP. 1650-90

RING AND DUTCH DROP 1690 ~ 1710

LOOP WITH BACK PLATE 1720 ~ 1740

FRETTED BACK PLATE C. 1750

GEORGIAN PLAIN LOOP 1750 ~ 1790

SHERATON CAST BRASS KNOB. 1790 ~ 1810

EMPIRE AND REGENCY 1810 ~ 30

LATE REGENCY ~ WILLIAM IV C. 1830

BOXES AND CONTAINERS

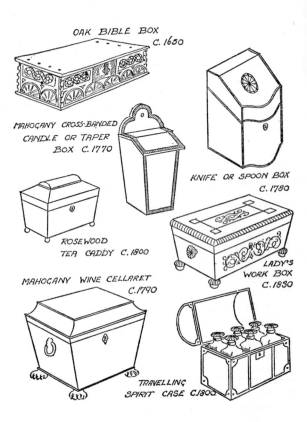

OAK BIBLE BOX C. 1650

MAHOGANY CROSS-BANDED CANDLE OR TAPER BOX C. 1770

KNIFE OR SPOON BOX C. 1780

ROSEWOOD TEA CADDY C. 1800

LADY'S WORK BOX C. 1830

MAHOGANY WINE CELLARET C. 1790

TRAVELLING SPIRIT CASE C. 1800

CHAPTER 4

Tables, Dressers and Sideboards

Medieval boards and trestles—survival of the term "board"—
the Tudor refectory table—pull-out or draw-leaf tables—the credence and origin of the gate-leg table—long period of the gate-leg—
occasional joined tables—18th-century patterns with club legs—
the composite "D" end table—tripod tea tables with dished and
pie-crust tops—dating by shape of feet—early games tables—18th-
century card tables—Sheraton quartetto or nest tables—variations
of the Pembroke style—sofa tables and early 19th-century folding
tables—early dressers—dressers developed from side tables—
Welsh dressers—appearance of the sideboard—Victorian chiffoniers.

In the communal life of medieval times the servant ate
with his master and his place at the table was a kind of
status symbol. The master would sit at the head with his
guests and family; next would come the retainers of
importance such as the steward and the priest and finally
the servants. Accordingly the table was a very long one and
as the great hall was also used for recreation and even for
sleeping the table had to be constructed so that, in spite of
its size, it could be easily dismantled and put to one side
when not required.

Tables of the Gothic period were referred to as boards
and trestles and were made in a variety of styles. Sometimes the supports were as those illustrated in the Luttrell
Psalter and later they took the form of pedestals. Until
the middle of the 16th century the table top consisted of a
massive board of oak or elm boards nailed together. When
laid over the trestles or pedestals the very weight preserved
its stability. Even to this day, landladies advertise "board

and lodging" and we still speak of a board of directors, a board room and a board of governors. It is interesting to note how this term, used to describe a council of men and women meeting around a table, is a survival in our language from a very distant past.

By 1550 the communal life of the hall had begun to disappear. Houses were being built with a greater number of rooms and master and man took their meals apart. There was no longer a need for the long trestle table and so a smaller table with a permanent underframe and legs was taken into general use. It was probably a smaller adaptation of the joined tables used in the abbey refectories and nowadays the term, refectory table, is used to describe it, although it was a purely domestic piece of furniture.

The refectory table, which was in everyday use from about 1550 to 1660, was usually 8 to 12 feet in length. It was stoutly constructed with four, six or eight legs with bottom rails between them, and the top permanently fixed. The underframing was made of oak but the top was often of elmwood, because of the wide boards which could be obtained from that tree.

During the reign of Elizabeth I a variant of the refectory table, known as a draw-leaf table, appeared on the scene. It enabled a comparatively short table to be extended to nearly twice its length by pulling out under-leaves from both ends. It was a design introduced from Flanders and France and it enjoyed an equal popularity with the refectory table. Both of these types were displaced by the gate leg table after the Restoration but the draw-leaf table ha been revived during the 20th century and many modern homes possess similar, but lighter versions of the Elizabethan prototype.

During the second half of the 16th and the early years of the 17th centuries, table legs were massively made and often took the form of heavy bulbous turnings. On Flemish tables these swollen shapes are often spherical, like a melon, but the English versions were considerably more elongated with rounded tops and bottoms. It has been said that these bulbous legs were functional in that they were designed to prevent rats climbing on to the table tops. I have it on good authority from a biologist friend that any self-respecting rat could easily leap on to a table without any climbing aids.

Between 1600 and 1630, a small but sturdily constructed kind of side table was developed. It must be considered a somewhat rare example of early Stuart furniture as examples these days are seldom encountered. The table-top was of the folding type, that is, it consisted of two halves hinged together and normally kept closed. When required for use, the upper leaf would be opened outwards and this would be supported by a fifth leg, which could be swung out as in a gate-leg table. Actually, this small table was the forerunner of the gate-leg pattern. It is sometimes referred to as a *credence table*, which was placed at the side of the altar in the churches and on which the wine vessels and plate were arranged for use in the Communion service.

The gate-leg table, as already mentioned in Chapter 1, became generally fashionable after the Restoration and, in one form or another it is the one type of table which has been in continuous service ever since. Usually made with a gate on each side, some larger tables are to be found with quadruple gates. These were of the period when spiral twist legs were in vogue and were made of walnut or, occasionally, of oak.

A small type of side table, with a drawer and bobbin turned or baluster legs, must have been made in large numbers towards the end of the 17th century as they are frequently to be found in sale-rooms and antique shops. The finer versions are sometimes veneered and have curved stretchers as illustrated in Chapter 2. A more common and probably country-made variety is the so-called tavern table with its top overhanging the ends to a more than usual degree. The drawers of these tables are sometimes found with joiner's slides on the sides.

After being generally adopted as a dining table during the Restoration period, the gate-leg table was given a variety of leg shapes over the next hundred years. Baluster and spiral twists gave place to scrolled legs and eventually to a type of cabriole shape known as the club leg. Except for use on extending card tables, the cabriole leg was not ideally suited to larger table design, but the club leg variation remained in vogue until the introduction of the Chippendale square leg and the tapered legs of the Adam and Hepplewhite eras.

It was customary during the late Stuart and William and Mary periods for a host to seat his guests at several gate-leg dining tables if the company was a large one. By the mid-18th century, however, long mahogany dining tables at which all the company could be seated, began to appear in the more important households. For over fifty years, these long dining tables consisted of one or several gate-leg tables, with rectangular side-leaves, which were joined together and semi-circular "D" end tables were placed at each end to make up the piece. The wide mahogany boards, introduced during the previous decades, rendered the construction of the broad table-tops a relatively simple matter.

When only a few people were at dinner, the "D" ends would be placed against the wall to serve as side tables and only the gate-leg would be in use. These "D" end tables are quite often to be seen in antique shops, either singly or in pairs, and it is not always realised that they have originally been part of a long Georgian dining table. When placed together, a pair of these tables make a very attractive circular dining table, which would be admirably suited to a present-day flat or smaller modern house. The long "D" end tables continued in use well into the 19th century but the tapered legs were in time replaced by centre pedestals, each supported on four long curved feet. These were usually reeded and had brass-capped ends with castors or brass leopard-paw ends.

Designed during the closing years of the 17th century, but not becoming generally popular until fifty years later, the small, snap-top, tripod table with a circular top is probably one of the commonest pieces of antique furniture to be found today. The hinged top of the simpler country-made examples is usually flat but a tea table with a dished or slightly hollow top is not uncommon. The dished top was designed to prevent spilt tea or milk running over on to the carpet. A more elaborate type of the dished top was known as a pie crust. Here the edge was carved into a series of scallop shapes, but genuine pie-crust tops are rare and there are many reproductions about. Some tripod tea tables have an open, box-like structure fitted underneath, known as a birdcage and into which the single, central pillar is made to fit. With this device, the table top not only folds upwards but can also be rotated so that any dish upon the table may be brought within reach of the guests.

It is possible to date a tripod table, to within twenty years, by the shape of the feet. As illustrated on p. 63, the feet of around 1750 to 1770 have a flatter curve with a wider spread, while those of 1770 to 1790 have a more pronounced hump at the knee. From 1790 to 1810 approximately, the curve of the feet was reversed and by the time of the Regency, slender, concave shaped feet had been introduced. The early Victorian period saw the revival of the "S" shape, but this was usually rather thick in proportion and decorated with elaborate carving.

Tables which were specially designed for playing games were rare during the 17th century but an interesting piece, known as a shuffleboard table, is sometimes to be found in the long galleries of our greater country houses. The long galleries were built for leisure and relaxation so that during the winter months, while the gentlemen went hunting, the ladies could take more gentle exercise indoors. The shuffleboard table can best be compared with a shove-ha'penny board, save that large brass discs were used instead of coins and the table top was often very long. There is one at Astley Hall in Lancashire which has twenty stout legs and is 27½ feet long. It must have been prefabricated and then assembled in the long gallery as it is far too large ever to have been brought up the staircase in one piece.

During the reign of Queen Anne and the Georgian period, card games were extremely popular and folding top tables with cabriole legs were in general use during that time. These tables were mostly made of walnut and had small recesses near the edges of the top to hold the guineas or counters while small circular platforms were provided at each corner to hold candlesticks for the night's play.

Card tables and tea tables, particularly the folding, semi-circular variety with tapered legs, were made to an almost identical pattern, the only difference being that the games tables had inset baize tops while the tea tables were of polished wood. The early 19th century saw the production of many small games tables with tops inlaid for chess and backgammon and with drawers beneath to hold the apparatus for the games.

To Sheraton must be given the credit of designing the nest of tables, the idea for which appeared in his *Cabinet Directory* in 1803. The nest comprises four small, separate tables which all fit one under another. They were originally referred to as *quartetto* tables and being very lightly constructed and somewhat fragile, it is uncommon to find an original, complete set of four. Luckily, I have such a set in my possession which I believe was made by Gillow of Lancaster. It was salvaged from a second-hand furniture shop, the tables being scattered around among the jumble and the shopkeeper having no idea, apparently, that they formed a unique set.

Small Pembroke tables with side flaps supported by hinged brackets and said to have been designed originally at the request of the Duchess of Pembroke for occasional use, appeared about 1775. They were common in late Georgian homes and in the early part of the 19th century a larger version was made to serve as a supper or breakfast table.

Sofa tables were designed to stand behind a sofa and to carry such things as reading and writing matter, trays of refreshments and candelabras. A few years ago, they were fairly common but are now in such great demand as bedroom dressing tables, that they have become a somewhat rare and expensive item.

The Regency and early Victorian periods saw a vast number of tables with folding tops, made to stand on a central pedestal with three or four feet. In this type, the double top, when opened out, could be rotated so that it was supported by a rectangular underframing. These tables were used for games, writing, serving tea and a whole host of leisure activites.

A necessary adjunct to every dining room is a sideboard and to every kitchen or living room, a dresser. The sideboard, as its name implies, was a small side table in those far off days when a dining table was referred to as a board. As the piece of furniture we know, it did not appear until the second half of the 18th century. The dresser, on the other hand, is of far more ancient lineage and in the painting of the More family by Holbein, referred to in Chapter

1, there is shown in the background a high-backed, cano-pied Gothic dresser, or, as it was called in that period, a *dressoir*. These dressers were really related to the cup-board or buffet and further reference will be made to them in the chapter on Cupboards.

Dressers with a high back were out of fashion during the early Stuart and Commonwealth times but there were two simpler types in general use. One was made in the form of a long, narrow side table with three or four deep drawers. It stood on four or six legs and had an under shelf, as wide as the dresser top, near the floor level. This was, no doubt, used for the display of brass and copper ware. The other type was a development of the chest and presented a more solid appearance, the entire front being filled with drawers and small cupboards. This second kind of dresser was not generally adopted until after the Restoration but both types were used then until the end of the 17th century.

By the beginning of the Georgian period most dressers were fitted with a set of plate shelves which stood at the rear of the dresser top. This version was usually referred to as a Welsh dresser and while it may have been popular in the Welsh farmhouse kitchen, it was undoubtedly made throughout Britain during the 18th and 19th centuries. Occasionally dressers are found made in walnut but more frequently in oak with the edges of the drawer fronts and the cupboard doors cross-banded in walnut or mahogany.

Long sidetables were normally used as sideboards in early Georgian dining rooms and on these would be placed the knife and fork boxes with the cellaret for wines underneath. It was about 1775 that the first sideboards were designed with drawers for the silver and cutlery and deep cupboards on either side to hold the wines. Sheraton is supposed to have added the low brass rail with a small silk curtain at the back to the designs for bow-fronted sideboards, which had originated during the Hepplewhite period.

In Victorian times, some monstrous sideboards were created with the addition of the most elaborate carving. In the great dining room at Charlecote Park, near Stratford upon Avon, there is installed such a piece of furniture with carved effigies of every variety of edible fish, animal and fowl hanging in great swags from every point and corner. This monument to the questionable good taste of the Victorians is all meticulously worked in varnished oak, a spectacle which must have made the shade of Grinling Gibbons sadly shake its head.

On the other hand, it was during the mid-Victorian period that a very attractive little sideboard, known as a *chiffonier*, made its appearance. It was equally useful as a sideboard for a small dining room or as a cabinet for a drawing room. Made in mahogany or veneered with burr walnut, it was certainly one of the more commendable inspirations of the designers during the Victorian era.

TRESTLE TABLE AS DEPICTED
IN THE LUTTRELL PSALTER C.1350

ELIZABETHAN
DRAW~LEAF TABLE
C.1575

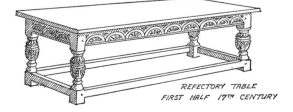

REFECTORY TABLE
FIRST HALF 17TH CENTURY

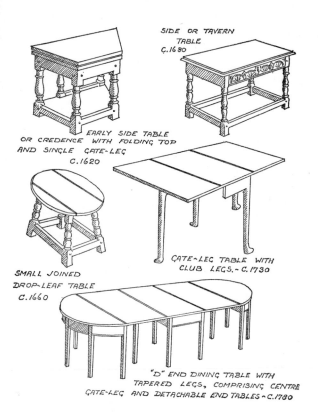

SIDE OR TAVERN
TABLE
C.1680

EARLY SIDE TABLE
OR CREDENCE WITH FOLDING TOP
AND SINGLE GATE-LEG
C.1620

SMALL JOINED
DROP-LEAF TABLE
C.1660

GATE-LEG TABLE WITH
CLUB LEGS.~ C.1730

"D" END DINING TABLE WITH
TAPERED LEGS, COMPRISING CENTRE
GATE-LEG AND DETACHABLE END TABLES ~ C.1780

TUDOR DRESSOIR
C. 1530

STUART DRESSER
C. 1640

SHERATON BOW FRONT
SIDEBOARD C. 1800

WELSH DRESSER
C. 1775

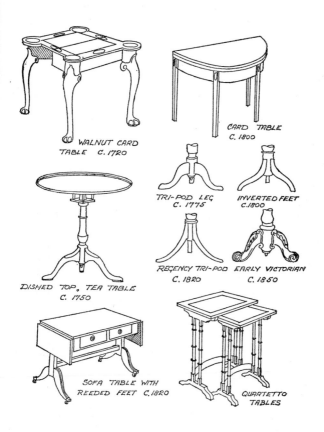

WALNUT CARD TABLE C. 1720

CARD TABLE C. 1800

TRI-POD LEG C. 1775

INVERTED FEET C. 1800

DISHED TOP, TEA TABLE C. 1750

REGENCY TRI-POD C. 1820

EARLY VICTORIAN C. 1850

SOFA TABLE WITH REEDED FEET C. 1820

QUARTETTO TABLES

CHAPTER 5

Stools, Chairs and Settees

Early forms of stools—development of the chair—scarcity of chairs before the 17th century—etiquette of the joined stool—upholstered farthingale chairs—"monk seats" and Commonwealth chairs—Restoration chair design—characteristics of William and Mary chairs—Queen Anne cabriole legs and the fiddle splat—wing chairs—Chippendale chair designs—chair backs of Hepplewhite—Adam's classical shapes—Sheraton elegance—Regency and early Victorian chairs—the mystery of the Windsor chair—harlequin sets—the emergence of the settle—love seats and the development of the settee.

On a marble panel in Athens which dates from around 400 B.C. a woman is to be seen seated on a chair which has all the characteristics of a British chair of the Regency period. The designers of Regency furniture, like Thomas Hope and Henry Moses, went to the ancient civilisations for their inspiration and this chair in the Athenian sculpture is an interesting case of "it has all happened before".

After the disorders of the Dark Ages when so much of art and craftsmanship was lost, the way of making beautiful and serviceable things had to be rediscovered or reinvented. At the beginning of the early Tudor period it can be said that in any house, even of the greatest importance, most people had to be content to sit on stools. Sometimes these were of the planked type as illustrated in Chapter 1, but more often they were made of turned wood with triangular shaped seats. This type of stool was common throughout northern Europe and when they are encountered it is difficult to say what may have been their country of origin.

Small chests were also used as seats in early times and formed one of the sources from which the chair developed, the other being the triangular-seated stool. In both these instances the need to provide additional support for the body brought about the addition of backs and arms to the stools. The first box or chest chairs were very heavy and cumbersome and it became evident that there was little advantage in constructing chairs in this way. For a short while [this type of chair was made without the lower side and back panels but with the front panel still included. By the middle of the 16th century the oak arm-chair, without any lower panels in the framework, was to be found in most houses of the reasonably well-to-do.

A custom, lasting for many years, delayed the employment of the chair for general use. During the second half of the 16th and for the greater part of the 17th century it was commonly accepted that only the head of the family or the master of the house should occupy a chair. In some homes a thoughtful husband might provide a chair for his wife but as for the rest of the household, they had to use stools or remain standing. The modern word chairman, to denote the head of a committee, is probably derived from this ancient practice. On a point of etiquette, observed in Britain during the 17th century, a host and his wife would vacate their chairs when entertaining an important guest and would sit on joined stools, as a mark of deference, while the guest occupied a chair.

The heavy oak arm-chair of the late Elizabethan and the early Stuart periods was of very much the same pattern with turned legs and a carved or inlaid panel in the chair-back. The only marked difference in construction was in the top rail of the back. While the Elizabethan chair had the top rail jointed between the uprights, the Stuart version had the uprights jointed into the top rail which projected at the sides and was supported by "ears" or small brackets.

The joined stool must have been made in considerable numbers during the 17th century as it was frequently referred to in bequests and inventories. Nowadays, it is sometimes called a *coffin stool* which is rather a misnomer. It is true that in many old churches joined stools are to be found carrying piles of hymn books or collecting boxes and occasionally they may have been used for supporting a coffin during a burial service, but they were certainly not designed for that purpose. A joined stool was the average person's seat in the 17th-century household, either at the dining table or around the fire. It is likely that those found in old churches today were banished there from the vicarage when custom and funds permitted the parson to provide himself with the more comfortable chairs.

While chairs with wooden seats were in use throughout the 17th century and also during the 18th in the houses of country-folk, upholstered chairs did appear in the early Stuart period. These, like the farthingale chairs, have already been mentioned in a previous chapter but during the Commonwealth somewhat heavy oak dining chairs were taken into use about the same time as the gate-leg table appeared. These were similar to the farthingale chairs but had lower seats and higher backs which were upholstered in thick leather and edged with large brass round-headed nails.

An interesting, dual-purpose piece of furniture was developed about this time. Known as a *table-chair*, it was constructed so that when the table-top was tilted to a vertical position it formed the back of a chair. It is sometimes referred to as a *monk's seat*, but the Dissolution of the Monasteries and the consequent banishment of the monks from the British way of life had occurred over a hundred years before the table-chair was invented.

The chief characteristic of Restoration chair design was the spiral twist for legs and backs. A favourite motif of the wood-carver for chair decoration was the device of two cherubs, or *amorini*, supporting a royal crown. This was inspired by the return of the monarchy after the Commonwealth and remained in popular favour until the close of the century. Chairs of the better quality were usually made in walnut but in the provinces many dining chairs were produced in oak. Two varieties of these are usually referred to as Yorkshire and Lancashire chairs. They were quite heavily made and the former had two shaped and rounded back-rails, decorated with carving and bearing a small bearded mask. Traditionally, this was said to represent the death mask of the martyred Charles I and earned for this Yorkshire type the name of *mortuary chair*. The Lancashire chairs, on the other hand, have panelled backs and I have an example in my possession on which the carving is very similar to that on a set in the ancient Chetham's School, Manchester, which dates from the mid-17th century. The finials on the uprights of my chair are the same as those on a settle which appears in Brueghel's painting *The Village Wedding*. The Brueghel picture was painted about 1530 and so we realise the slow movement of continental influence showing itself in the north of England over a hundred years later.

Portuguese and Spanish characteristics, entering England directly through royal marriages or more deviously through France and the Netherlands, considerably affected the design of William and Mary chairs. Here is found the tall, narrow back and the scrolled foot which during the reign of Queen Anne was to develop into the cabriole leg. On these chairs the design of the upper back rail is often repeated in the lower front rail.

The type of chair which evolved during the first decade of the 18th century was very pleasing to the eye. The first cabriole legs were quite plain but the chair-makers of the time did not consider that the chair legs were sufficiently strong to be made without connecting stretchers. However, by introducing a deeper seat rail it became possible to make a stronger joint at the top of the chair leg and eventually the stretchers were dispensed with altogether. The chair-backs of the Queen Anne period were of a pleasantly rounded appearance with a fiddle-shaped central splat, curved to support the sitter's back.

During the early Georgian period the cabriole leg remained in favour and without the stretchers was more sturdily fashioned than the finer Queen Anne shape. Moreover, it became the custom in the better class of chair to ornament the knees of the cabriole legs with carved shells, acanthus leaves or satyr masks. Instead of a simple pad at the bottom of the leg, the ball and claw foot was adopted. This was a pattern derived from a Chinese dragon motif which clasped in its claw a celestial pearl. All-over upholstery of chair backs now became fashionable, but it was a vogue which died out when Chippendale and his contemporaries introduced the elaborately carved chair backs of the mid-18th century.

Chippendale included a straight, square sectioned leg among the designs for his chairs and when made in the Chinese taste these were covered in low-relief carving to simulate lattice work. As if there was some doubt as to the structural efficiency of these legs, the use of stretchers was re-introduced. Chair backs were generally rectangular, whether the style was Gothic, Chinese or one of the many rococo patterns which decorated the pierced splats. Some of these complicated designs from Chippendale's *Director* were rather pleasingly simplified by country craftsmen, e.g. the well-known rush-seated ladder-back chair.

Around the beginning of the 18th century the wing-back chairs appeared, the earlier types having low, outwardly curving upholstered arms and cabriole feet. Later in the century the arms were made more upright and the side wings larger. The wing-chair is deceptive both in size and comfort. It often looks smaller than it really is and care should be taken before buying one to ensure that it will really fit in wherever it is intended to go. Although the winged chair marked a great advance in human comfort at the time, the unsprung seating feels hard compared with the resilience of 20th-century upholstery.

While George Hepplewhite was known to have made a considerable quantity of furniture to the designs of Robert Adam, he himself was probably responsible for many well-known types of chair such as the shield-back, the oval-back and the feathers pattern. The backs of Hepplewhite's chairs were more rounded than those of his predecessors and he also favoured tapered legs which were often fluted. His furniture generally was of a lighter appearance than that which had gone before. Sets of dining chairs usually consisted of ten or twelve single chairs and two arm-chairs or *carvers*. These latter were designed to accommodate the broad figures and full frock coats of the 18th-century gentlemen and the seats were made proportionately wide. The curve and sweep of the arms is also noteworthy for they were cut from solid blocks of mahogany of a size which would make it uneconomic to employ in modern reproductions.

Robert Adam designed his chairs to match the classical interior decoration of the houses he built. They had turned and fluted or tapered legs and the lyre-back pattern was typical. He contrived some elegant gilded chairs whose backs were adorned with small painted medallions on which appeared figures from Greek and Roman mythology. These were painted by contemporary artists like Angelica Kauffmann and Zucchi. Adam also introduced the fashion for painted beechwood furniture, and chairs in this style were often finished in black or white paint, neatly lined with gilding.

For some time previously gilded furniture had enjoyed considerable popularity. It is said that it was first introduced according to the wishes of the wives of those Georgian gentlemen who were filling their Palladian mansions with the rich but somewhat sombre mahogany furniture. Quite a large proportion of this gilded furniture was imported from France and it is very difficult to identify English made chairs from the French originals. French chairs are believed to have upholstered pads on the arms and small peg-like ends to the scrolled feet while English gilded chairs are supposed not to have had any upholstery on the arms while the scrolls reached right down to the end of the legs. I have, however, seen both English and French chairs with variations of all these characteristics.

The rectangular chair-back returned with Thomas Sheraton, who of all the 18th-century designers could probably claim to have the greatest delicacy of taste. He owed this success to a lightness of construction, hitherto unattained, and to his use of the natural beauty of the mahogany and satinwood grain. This he left without embellishment except for a slight amount of inlay and some boxwood stringing along the edges. Sheraton was very close to the 20th century in his chair designs and I have seen dining chairs produced by well-known designers of the present day where the influence of Thomas Sheraton has been very strong indeed.

Regency chairs have a distinctive elegance of their own, and although they could be bought quite cheaply in sets before the 1939-45 War, today they are very much in demand. They are rather simply shaped with slender, turned legs and attractively scrolled backs. The back rails are often inlaid with ebony or brass and the lower rail is sometimes found carved like a rope length. It was during this period that the top back rail was constructed so that it protruded on either side of the uprights, this design often being associated with the so-called *sabre-shaped leg*.

The Restoration spiral twist now re-appeared in the Abbotsford furniture of the early Victorian period. These chairs were usually made of walnut or rosewood but could never be mistaken for late 17th-century pieces. In spite of their rather fussy character and beadwork upholstery they are attractive and well worth acquiring. About 1860 the cabriole leg returned to favour and many sets of attractive chairs, designed for the drawing room or parlour, were produced. Country-made rush-seated chairs with turned spindle backs and club legs date from the early 19th century and are still made in some northern counties.

The origin of the Windsor chair is shrouded in mystery, as is also the name. The tale that George III discovered this turned-wood type of chair at a house in the Chilterns and found it so to his liking that he had it sent to Windsor for his personal use may be accepted with that degree of credulity accorded to many fables concerning antiques. Some authorities date the Windsor chair from the late 17th century and others from the mid-18th. It is more than likely that in areas such as the Chilterns, where there are extensive beech forests, turned-wood stools and chairs have been produced for a very long time, even as far back as the 16th century. The Windsor chair as it is known to-day was really a product of the 18th century and it was probably during that time that it reached that very high degree of functional design for which it has become famous. Traditionally, these chairs have legs and spindles of beech which until a short time ago were shaped on crude lathes in the beechwoods by turners known as *bodgers*. The hooped backs and arms were made of ash which could be easily steamed and bent to shape while the seats were of elm because they could be cut in one piece from the broad elm boards. Some Windsor chairs have yew-wood arms, backs and spindles but are rather more rare and consequently more expensive to acquire. Those which have a shaped central splat in the back with a small wheel-like figure incorporated in the design are usually referred to as wheel-back chairs.

I have already mentioned sets of Georgian dining chairs and these command a high price, even when country-made. Due to a 19th-century custom of dividing sets of chairs among the beneficiaries of the will on the death of the owner, it is quite common to find single specimens or pairs of chairs of almost any period in sale-rooms and antique shops. Accordingly, it is not a difficult matter to collect what is sometimes referred to by the antique trade as a *harlequin set* of different chairs, either of the same or various periods. In my dining room I have a very pleasant example of the Hepplewhite period, a pair and one single chair of Sheraton design, and two Regency carvers. None of these cost more than £5 and some much less.

High-backed oak settles look cosy and attractive before an open fire in a country inn but they are not really very comfortable and seldom fit in with a modest collection of antique furniture. They often have a chest beneath with a hinged lid in the seat and sometimes shaped wings at the sides to combat the draughts. The low-back settle or panelled settee with cabriole legs and a long overlaid cushioned seat are a better proposition and can be bought for under £10.

Of much rarer vintage is the double seated settee or *love seat*, designed according to tradition for the use of courting couples. I believe that this is just another fable as these seats are not infrequently found in pairs, the second one provided, perhaps, for the chaperone. More likely these love seats were merely part of the seating accommodation provided in a large salon or ballroom for the assemblies and routs so much beloved by the Georgians.

Longer settees with cabriole or square Chippendale type legs, and with padded arms and upholstered seats and backs, made an appearance in the second half of the 18th century. Apparently they did not develop in popularity as there are comparatively few about and their places were taken by the sofa and couch.

EARLY CHAIRS

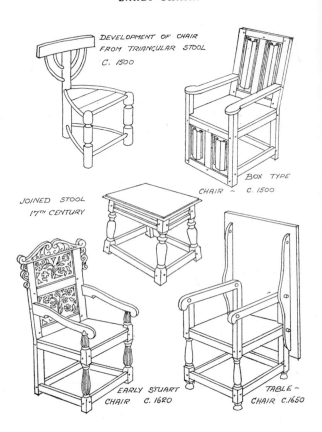

DEVELOPMENT OF CHAIR
FROM TRIANGULAR STOOL
C. 1500

BOX TYPE
CHAIR ~ C. 1500

JOINED STOOL
17TH CENTURY

EARLY STUART
CHAIR C. 1620

TABLE ~
CHAIR C.1650

YORKSHIRE
CHAIR ~ C. 1650

LANCASHIRE
CHAIR ~ C. 1650

WILLIAM AND MARY CHAIR
WITH SCROLLED LEGS
C. 1690

QUEEN ANNE CHAIR
C. 1710

GEORGE I
CHAIR ~ WITH
ALL OVER UPHOLSTERY   C. 1720

CHIPPENDALE CARVER

WING CHAIR   C. 1775

GOTHIC REVIVAL

CHINESE TASTE

RIBBON BACK

ADAM LYRE BACK

HEPPLEWHITE OVAL BACK

SHERATON CHAIR
C. 1800

REGENCY CARVER
C. 1825

ROMANTIC
(ABBOTSFORD) REVIVAL
C. 1840

MID-VICTORIAN
C. 1860

WINDSOR
CHAIR
18TH CENT

OAK SETTLE
C. 1670

COUNTRY MADE ~
PANEL BACK
SETTEE C. 1730

LOVE ~ SEAT OR
SMALL SETTEE
C. 1730

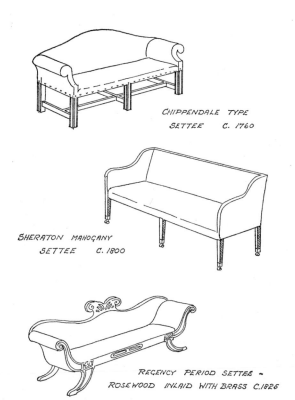

CHIPPENDALE TYPE
SETTEE   C. 1760

SHERATON MAHOGANY
SETTEE   C. 1800

REGENCY PERIOD SETTEE –
ROSEWOOD INLAID WITH BRASS C.1825

CHAPTER 6

Cupboards, Wardrobes and Small Hanging Cupboards

Evolution of the cupboard—development from a chest form—the Gothic hutch or livery cupboard—origin of the "cup board" or buffet—the court cupboard and press—lasting popularity in Wales of the deuddarn and tridarn—armoires, cloak cupboards and the linen press—later appearance of the wardrobe—hanging dole and medicine cupboards—various fronts of the corner cupboard—painted interiors—Victorian buffets.

The cupboard may have evolved from a chest form because a chest, when placed on its end, would serve as a narrow cupboard or locker. Again, the chest on legs with an overhanging top and hinged doors beneath, like the counter mentioned in Chapter 3, could also have been an ancestor of the cupboard.

The counter was sometimes referred to as a *hutch* in old documents but nowadays the latter name is usually only given to a wired cage for tame rabbits. In the Gothic period the hutch was a small planked cupboard used chiefly as a food larder. The door and front were perforated with frets of an architectural character to allow air to circulate and so keep the food fresh. Pieces of loosely woven horse-hair were nailed to the inside of the frets to keep flies and insects away from the contents. While the horse-hair has long since perished the remains of the small nails which held it in position are sometimes still to be seen.

Many books on antique furniture show an illustration of Prince Arthur's Cupboard, which is in the Victoria and Albert Museum. It dates from around 1500 and is one of the finest pieces of English Gothic furniture in existence. It is unique and the chances of discovering a similar piece are negligible. However, it is possible that the smaller planked hutch, although very rare, may still be found by the discerning seeker after antique oak. I know of one in the possession of a Cotswold antique dealer but he says that £1,000 would not buy it. On the other hand, there are a considerable number of hutches at Haddon Hall in Derbyshire. In that part of the house open to public view I have counted nearly a score, so it is not beyond a reasonable possibility that there are hutches lying in old barns and attics elsewhere which might turn up one day and offer themselves to a knowing buyer.

Apparently, it was a custom in the Middle Ages to keep a small supply of food in private rooms for use at any time. This would be stored in hutches which in time came to be referred to as livery cupboards. This term was in use until a few years ago and I remember an inn near my home where there was a painted notice over the entrance to the inn-yard, now given over to car parking, which bore the legend "livery and bait". This indicated that change of horses and refreshments for the journey were always readily available.

Aumbry is another old name for a hutch or livery cupboard. There are some antiquaries, however, who maintain that the aumbry was not a standing cupboard but was essentially a recess in a wall which was enclosed by a door in a frame. It may be that in different times the word was used to describe several types of cupboard.

The "cup board" proper was originally a side table or buffet which was a fitment with two or three shelves made to stand against the wall in the proximity of the dining table. On this were kept the wooden trenchers or platters for use at meal times. In the 16th century and later it was used to display the silver or pewter table-ware, according to the opulence of the household.

Early buffets vary in the amount of decoration, some being merely a set of shelves with some simple carving on the rails supporting the shelves. Others were larger and more elaborate with bulbous turnings on the front uprights and sometimes the centre and top rails concealed long shallow drawers which fitted under the shelves. These were used for storing spoons and knives only as forks had not been adopted for table use at this time.

Towards the end of the Elizabethan period it became the practice to construct buffets with the upper staging enclosed with panels and doors. This piece of furniture was known as a court cupboard from the French word *court*, meaning short or low. Eventually, the lower stage of the court cupboard was enclosed as well during the early years of the 17th century and the cupboard form became really established from then onward. In recent years the term court cupboard has been quite often misapplied to these completely enclosed cupboards. The late R. W. Symonds, who was probably one of the most authoritative furniture historians of the 20th century, has been able to confirm by much diligent research into old house inventories and wills that the correct name is actually a press.

The press was invariably made in oak and a considerable number were produced during the 17th century. They were built as a rule with three tiers of cupboard doors showing on the front, two doors being on each of the top and middle tiers and one on the bottom. The rails were decorated with low-relief strapwork carving and ornamental mouldings were sometimes applied to the panels and door frames. Carved initials of the owner and his wife, together with a date to commemorate some family happening, were favourite additions to the design. Many of these cupboards had large pendant turnings on either side of the overhanging top. These were the vestiges of the original bulbous turnings used on the front uprights of the buffet and court cupboard. The small doors are, for the most part, found with wrought-iron butterfly hinges but early presses had upper doors which turned on wooden dowel pins. Small turned wooden knobs were used as handles on the door frames.

The early press was essentially a cupboard for storing food and table-ware and should not be confused with the linen press of the following century, details of which will be given later in the chapter. For the most part it was of fairly large size being 6 to 8 feet in length and would have been found in the dining or living rooms of the more prosperous Stuart and Commonwealth farmers. Consequently, it can seldom be accommodated in a present-day house.

However, there are smaller and rather attractive versions of the press which were made in Wales and enjoyed a degree of popularity during the 18th century, although the press in England had been superseded by the dresser. These Welsh pieces were of two very similar types and were known as the *deuddarn* and *tridarn*, the former being constructed with two tiers or stages only while the latter had three. The top tier of the tridarn is seldom a fixture and can usually be lifted off, should this be necessary. These small press-type cupboards are seldom ornate but being comparatively small, often only 4 to 4½ feet in length, the breaking up of the front surface with doors and panelling permits the mellowness of the old oak to be appreciated to the full. In the deuddarn, drawers are sometimes included between the lower and upper tiers.

Tall cupboards for hanging clothes had been in use on the continent since the early 16th century. There they were referred to as *armoires* and it is thought that they were probably used for storing armour and weapons as well as clothes. The few early armoires to be found in

Britain are nearly always of French or Flemish origin, and cupboards designed for holding garments were rarely to be found in these islands until the beginning of the 18th century.

Hitherto, the accepted method of storing gowns and suits of clothes was to use a chest or a large chest of drawers. Now a large cupboard with double doors was adopted for the purpose. It was mounted on a chest of drawers but a closer examination of the two top drawers will show them to be merely false fronts which do not open. Behind them the space is used to afford greater hanging room for the clothes in the cupboard above. The lower drawers were made to function in the normal way. Before the invention of clothes hangers the contents of the cloak cupboard or clothes press were hung on a series of wooden pegs placed along the back and sides of the cupboard interior.

Sometimes, the cupboard space above the drawers was fitted with wide trays for the storage of linen. Although the exterior would be identical to that of a cloak cupboard, the article in this case would be called a linen press and the top drawers would be real ones as a deeper hanging space for clothes would not be necessary.

Taller wardrobes without dummy drawers were produced by Chippendale, Hepplewhite and other cabinet-makers. These were very elegant in appearance with finely veneered doors and sometimes with bow-fronts. In mid-Victorian times some huge wardrobes were constructed in three or four separate sections. These were screwed together when assembled in position and included bays for hanging clothes, long dressing mirrors and sections with trays for keeping linen wear. Today, these well-made mahogany and satinwood edifices are indeed white elephants for they are much too large ever to go into a modern house or flat. Usually they are bought very cheaply and then taken apart so that the fine wood in them can be used in the manufacture of reproduction pieces, sometimes advertised as "made from genuine old wood". I suppose that if one cannot acquire the authentic article then these are the next best thing.

Since the late 16th century, small hanging cupboards have always appeared among the more usual furnishings. Towards the end of the reign of Elizabeth I and in early Stuart times wall cupboards with fretted fronts or with the door frames filled with rows of baluster shaped spindles were in general use. Nowadays they are referred to as *dole*, or food, cupboards and were once hung inside churches to contain the bread doles provided by charity bequests. They were probably used as food larders in the kitchens of private houses as well. Although this cupboard form is rarely found as an antique in England these days it is not an uncommon discovery in Wales.

In the 17th and 18th centuries when doctors and apothecaries were few and far between, every housewife kept a store of medicinal herbs and remedies for administering to her family in times of sickness. These were preserved in small cupboards which hung on the wall or stood on a chest of drawers and contained a number of pigeon-holes and small drawers for separating the various herbs. I always regret having failed to acquire one of these little spice or herb cupboards which a dealer friend of mine had in the shop. Other dealers had passed it by, saying that it was only an old top from a grandfather clock which had been converted into a little cupboard. Actually, it was a genuine Queen Anne medicine cupboard with a finely panelled door and a neat compartment of drawers inside. However, the question had then arisen, as it does for all collectors sooner or later, of just where it was going to fit in with all the other things, and the opportunity had to be missed.

Corner cupboards, like tripod tables, are probably more

numerous than any other type of antique furniture and are still to be had very reasonably. They were in general use throughout the Georgian period and served many purposes. Nowadays a corner cupboard with the doors left open makes an attractive setting for a small collection of china or Staffordshire chimney ornaments. Oak corner cupboards are usually flat-fronted with canted corners but occasionally they are found with bow-fronts. This is the pattern which was more often adopted for the mahogany cupboard and with an inlaid frieze at the top and a couple of small drawers beneath, this would make a very desirable acquisition to any modest collection of antique furniture.

Some flat fronted corner cupboards have glazed, *astragal doors*, that is with little panes of glass set into a framework of thin bars or beads. These are usually original but a door with a single sheet of glass in it has probably had the wooden panel removed and glass substituted for the display of china or silver. Do not be in a hurry to strip or paint over if the interior of your cupboard is decorated in a faded olive green colour. This is probably the original finish as the Georgians were very fond of green linings to their cupboards and cabinets and a little toilet soap and warm water will most likely restore the paintwork very nearly to its original condition.

Finally, some mention should be made of the reappearance of the buffet in mid-Victorian dining rooms. Much lighter in design than its Tudor counterpart, it usually consisted of three quite deep shelves supported on four slim mahogany, turned corner uprights. These buffets, like the 17th-century press, are often too large for the modern house. Occasionally they are to be seen, laden with dish covers, cutlery and cruets, in the spacious dining rooms of those old-fashioned but comfortable coaching inns which have survived into the day of the motor car.

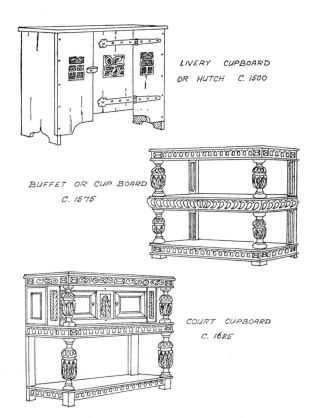

LIVERY CUPBOARD
OR HUTCH C. 1500

BUFFET OR CUP BOARD
C. 1575

COURT CUPBOARD
C. 1625

87

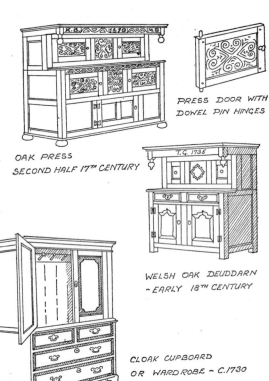

OAK PRESS
SECOND HALF 17TH CENTURY

PRESS DOOR WITH
DOWEL PIN HINGES

WELSH OAK DEUDDARN
- EARLY 18TH CENTURY

CLOAK CUPBOARD
OR WARDROBE ~ C.1730

HANGING CUPBOARDS

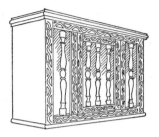

DOLE CUPBOARD ~
C. 1600

MEDICINE OR SPICE
CUPBOARD   C. 1710

BOW-FRONTED
CORNER CUPBOARD ~ C.1780

CORNER CUPBOARD WITH
GLAZED ASTRAGAL DOOR.
C. 1780

CHAPTER 7

Beds, Day-beds and Cradles

Early beds—rest for the rich and not-so-rich—misnomer of the
"four-poster"—characteristics of 17th-century bed construction—
development of the tester—beds of the mid-Georgian era—foreign
influences on late 18th-century bed design—truckle and folding
beds—origin of the day-bed—Restoration and early 18th-century
types—Regency elegance of the chaise-longue—the Victorian sofa—
cots and cradles.

Early beds were looked upon as the most important items
in any household. They were handed down from father to
son and were always mentioned with some degree of pride
of possession. They were often very heavy, monumental
constructions and the occupants depended for their
comfort on enormously thick, feather mattresses. These
were laid either on a network of ropes which passed
through holes in the framework or on a foundation of
wooden slats.

There must have been a general fear of draughts and
fresh air at night or the bedrooms were very cold and
draughty because it was the practice to enclose the beds
with panelling or heavy curtains until the end of the 18th
century. It is hardly likely that many people nowadays
would sleep in a 17th or 18th-century bed for choice,
although I have an old collector friend who nightly
repairs to his Georgian four-poster. I should add that it
has been fitted with a box-spring mattress of the latest
slumber-inducing design.

In medieval times the wealthy slept on free standing
frame beds overhung by a tent-like canopy which was

suspended from the ceiling. Servants and attendants slept on the floor or on straw palliasses. For information about beds in the time of Elizabeth I, we look again at William Harrison's *Description of England.* In it he wrote: "Our fathers have lain full often upon straw pallets, on rough mats covered with a sheet and a good round log under their heads for a pillow. If the goodman of the house had purchased a mattress or flock bed, and thereto a sack of chaff to rest his head upon, he thought himself to be as well lodged as the lord of the town, that peradventure lay seldom in a bed of down or whole feathers. As for servants, if they had any sheet above them, it was well, for seldom had they any under their bodies to keep them from the pricking straws that ran oft through the canvas of the pallet and rased their hardened hides."

The "four-poster" bed of antiquity is a well-known term but few have stopped to think that the four-poster, at any rate until the early Georgian period, was in fact only a two-poster, the back or bed-head which supported the top, or *tester*, being a panelled framework without posts. In the 17th century these beds were known as tester or posted beds. Medieval beds are so rare as to be almost non-existent but there are a number of beds with testers which can be dated from the late 16th century. Some of these were excessively large like the Great Bed of Ware, now in the Victoria and Albert Museum. It was made about 1595 and is 10 feet 9 inches wide. The great majority of beds, however, were between 5 and 6 feet in width.

Posted beds all followed a similar pattern, having a strong rectangular frame to carry the mattress and at the head a panelled screen, often elaborately decorated with carving and inlaid woods. This screen and two turned pillars at the foot of the bed supported a panelled ceiling or tester from which hung the curtains, to be drawn at night. The pillars at the bed-end were usually incorporated in the bed framework and acted as feet for the mattress framing. On larger beds, however, the framing would have separate feet and the posts supporting the tester would be free-standing on rectangular pedestal bases.

Some smaller beds were made with panelled screens erected at the bottom end as well as at the head so that they formed, in effect, large panelled boxes with curtained sides. They must have been very stuffy and altogether unhealthy. Whether it was a reaction against the unhygienic properties of the enclosed bed or just a simplification for economy's sake, a plainer type of bed appeared about the middle of the 17th century. It consisted merely of a framework on short legs and a low panelled bed-head. It is usually referred to as a farm-house bed. For those who have an ambition to equip their homes with antique furniture entirely, this type of bed, with a box-spring mattress fitted, can be quite an interesting acquisition. They are not uncommon and I have seen them from time to time in several sale-rooms.

The tester undoubtedly developed from the tent-like covering of the medieval bed and during the 16th and 17th centuries was a very heavy structure which demanded a strong supporting bed-framework. During the time of William and Mary and Queen Anne it became fashionable in the noble households to install beds which were most luxuriously appointed. In keeping with the tendency to build houses with higher ceilings to the rooms, these beds were also very high with elaborately decorated testers and the entire framework upholstered with quilted silk and velvet. Such beds were usually installed to commemorate the stay of some royal visitor.

Beds of the mid-18th century became altogether lighter in construction and appearance and although in some cases the bed-head screen to support the tester was retained, the more ordinary run of beds had lower bed-heads and four posts to support the tester. By this time the tester consisted only of four curtain poles placed across the tops of the posts with a light covering of material stretched over them. Thomas Chippendale made a bed for the Duke of Beaufort about 1750 in the Chinese taste. It has a pagoda-like top with flying dragons at the corners and, finished in black japan and gold, has a very attractive appearance. Another bed, painted in the Chinese manner, was made for David Garrick about 1770. It also has a light wooden tester with embroidered silk curtains and like the bed of the Duke of Beaufort indicates the tendency for greater delicacy in construction of furniture during the second half of the 18th century.

For some time during the 18th-century Italian and French beds were imported into the British Isles and although the numbers were small they influenced the design of the English type considerably. The Italians seem to have been the first to do away with the tester and its hangings. Probably in a warm climate common sense overruled fashion and tradition. French patterns of the late 18th century were very elaborate in the decoration of bed-heads and here also the tester seems to have been abandoned entirely. Only in England, and the climate was probably the chief reason for its retention, did the use of the tester linger on into the 19th century. Wooden canopies, from which side curtains were hung, were still being fitted over the bed-head about 1850.

Lightly constructed beds, rather like the folding kind used for camping today, became fairly common during the Georgian period. They were small enough to be kept under the posted beds when not required and were used by nurses or servants attending sick people or as extra accommodation for an unexpected visitor. I have seen small chests of drawers with dummy fronts which swung open like a cupboard door. Inside were folding beds which could be pulled out when wanted. All these lighter types were generally known as truckle beds and were fitted with small wheels or castors so that they could easily be moved around.

I have already mentioned in a previous chapter how chests were used as seats in early times and it is evident that the larger ones also served as beds or couches. Some years ago in a sale-room I saw a panelled oak chest with raised ends. Although I did not realise it at the time I had come across an *archebanc couchette*, probably of early French design which had been made to serve both as a chest and a couch. I have never seen another since and only hope that one day the opportunity to acquire such a rarity might present itself again.

From these bed-chests probably developed the more lightly constructed single bed or day-bed which appeared towards the end of the 16th century. Shakespeare has referred to them in his plays and, by the Restoration, day-beds had reached a pleasing standard of design. They were made in walnut with six or eight legs and had an adjustable end frame which, together with the main framework of the bed, was equipped with woven split-canework to give some resilience to the overlay cushions. Day-beds with double ends are found occasionally but they are very rare.

The day-bed continued in use throughout the 18th century conforming to the fashionable characteristics of the time, but it is rather difficult to separate its development into that form known as the chaise-longue from that of the settee, couch or sofa. Although all these types were used for lying or for sitting upon, I think it should be remembered that the day-bed was designed primarily for resting during the day-time while the settee or sofa was made to enable a number of people to sit together on the same seat. Perhaps the best way to remember the difference is that the day-bed or chaise-longue was never made with a back like a couch or a settee. In its later form, as used in the 19th and 20th centuries, it has become known as the divan having neither end supports nor back.

The chaise-longue of the late Georgian and Regency periods became the symbol of elegant repose, typified perhaps by Jacques Louis David's portrait of Madame Récamier. The beautiful piece of furniture with its gracefully curving ends was said to have been designed by the artist himself. It was in all probability among the finest of the adaptations by the late 18th and early 19th-century designers from the sources of classical Greece and Rome. A shorter form of seat which is often identical in appearance to the chaise-longue is the window seat. Like the former, it has no back but is too short for reclining upon and as its name implies was just a small seat made to fit into a low window bay without obscuring the view.

The type of Victorian sofa which has just the one scrolled end and a short back-piece running only half its length is really in the tradition of the day-bed rather than that of the couch or settee. Those made in walnut about 1850 with small cabriole legs are attractive pieces of furniture and become increasingly rare as time goes on.

Children's cots and cradles are really among the few antiques which are not normally put to their original use and would hardly be considered suitable for the modern baby. Nowadays, babies are put to bed and left to sleep or lie awake as they will but in olden times an essential of all cot and cradle design was that they should be able to be rocked. The two swinging cots illustrated have basically the same structure although they are separated by more than 300 years. The Gothic cot is just an oak box suspended from a well-made stand while the late Georgian version, dating from around 1820, is a much finer affair in turned and reeded mahogany. It has a clockwork mechanism incorporated in the suspension of the cot which will actually cause it to rock for nearly an hour. It might be that the steady ticking of the clockwork also acted as a further soporific.

The more homely cradle of the farmhouse and cottage had a small hood at one end. It was mounted on a pair of rockers so that the mother could rock the baby to sleep with her foot while her hands were busy with some sewing or the preparation of food.

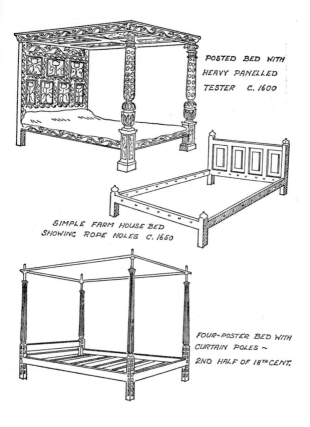

POSTED BED WITH
HEAVY PANELLED
TESTER C. 1600

SIMPLE FARM HOUSE BED
SHOWING ROPE HOLES C. 1650

FOUR-POSTER BED WITH
CURTAIN POLES ~
2ND HALF OF 18TH CENT.

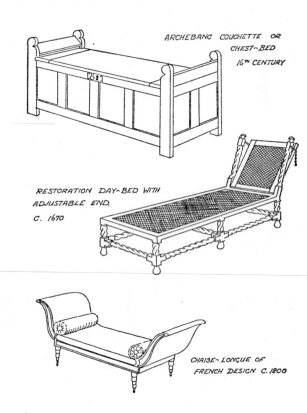

ARCHEBANC COUCHETTE OR CHEST-BED 16TH CENTURY

RESTORATION DAY-BED WITH ADJUSTABLE END. C. 1670

CHAISE-LONGUE OF FRENCH DESIGN C. 1800

SOFAS AND COTS

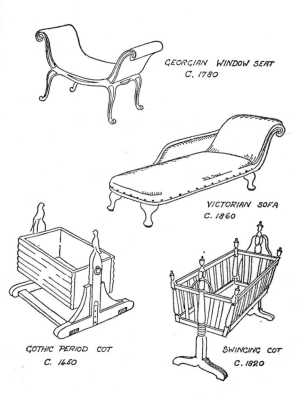

GEORGIAN WINDOW SEAT
C. 1780

VICTORIAN SOFA
C. 1860

GOTHIC PERIOD COT
C. 1450

SWINGING COT
C. 1820

CHAPTER 8

Desks, Bureaux, Bookcases and Cabinets

Table-desks—desks on stands—the fall-front scrutoire—development of the bureau—secret drawers—knee-hole and partners' desks—escritoires and military chests—boudoir desks and the "bonheur du jour"—19th-century davenports—Samuel Pepys and the first bookcases—the bureau bookcase and origins of the china cabinet—wall shelves and small standing bookcases.

Even in the 16th century life must have been starting to become a little complicated for the average individual. For the professional man and even for the farmer there were records to be kept and letters written and it was probably due to these facts that by the closing years of Elizabeth's reign small table-desks began to appear in many households. The steward and the merchant would have to employ a counter and chests as well but for the average man the table-desk was sufficient.

These small antique boxes, almost invariably constructed in oak, were very personal belongings and during the Stuart and Restoration periods it was the custom for the owner to have his name and some commemorative date carved upon the front. Although these table-desks vary in size from the rarer 3 feet in width to the more common 20 inches, they nearly all have the same basic construction. A box shape with a gently sloping lid, hinged with wrought-iron butterfly hinges, contains a small compartment of three drawers. A hasp lock was a normal addition.

These little desks are sometimes mistakenly referred to as bible boxes, as mentioned in Chapter 3. I think it was not unlikely that they contained the Bible in some homes, but there would have been little room left for documents accounts and valuables. I have a table-desk which belonged to a George Lowe who had his name and the date 1666, the year of the Great Fire of London, carved on the front. In it I keep a large bible which has been in my wife's family since the 17th century. The bible has the date 1668 imprinted with the dedication on the cover and it is an interesting coincidence that bible and desk should be so close together in time.

For anyone requiring an antique desk, it is possible to buy a table-desk for under £10 and placed on a small tavern type table with a drawer in the front they make an excellent substitute for the larger and far more expensive bureau. As a matter of fact, it was rather in this way that the bureau developed. During the latter years of the 17th century two types of desk were in evidence. There was the desk on a stand, which was a development of the table-desk, and a much larger and important piece of furniture called the secretary or *scrutoire*.

The desk on a stand marked an elementary but note-worthy stage in desk development. Hitherto it had been difficult to gain access to the contents of a desk when the desk lid was already covered with letters and documents. Accordingly, the hinges were changed over to the lower edge of the lid which now opened outwards and was in future referred to as the *desk-fall*. The fall was supported in the open position by pull-out battens called *lopers* and in some early stands it was the practice to incorporate two small gate-legs which could be swung out to support the fall instead of using lopers. The fitted interior of small drawers and added pigeon-holes was now much more accessible and it became possible to enlarge the number of drawers with the corresponding increase in the size of the desk.

The scrutoire was a much bigger item than the desk on a stand, being frequently over 5 feet in height. It consisted of a flat-fronted rectangular cabinet mounted on either a stand or a chest of drawers. The whole front of the scrutoire folded outwards and was supported by chains or metal stays. It offered a vastly bigger working area than the desk lid and contained many more drawers and compartments for holding documents and ledgers. Although used in the larger establishments with their corresponding need for more administrative storage space, the scrutoire enjoyed only a short existence and by 1700 was more or less obsolete. Strangely enough it returned to favour about 100 years later in a smaller and more compact form. It was produced in France during the post-Revolution Empire period and re-introduced into this country as the *secrétaire à abattant* or fall-front desk.

What is rather interesting now is that the furniture designers of the Queen Anne period took the better features of the desk on a stand and the scrutoire and incorporated them in a new form of desk which became known as a bureau. The early bureaux were made in two separate parts, the upper desk section being mounted on a base consisting of a chest of drawers. The sections were provided with carrying handles at the sides so that when being moved each part could be carried separately.

The fall was no longer supported by stays or gate-legs but by lopers. These were almost square in section in the earlier bureaux but by the middle of the 18th century it was found that lopers of greater depth were less likely to sag. Later desks have two small drawers instead of lopers which are pulled out to support the fall when in use. Another characteristic of early 18th-century bureaux was the well or space below the interior pigeon-hole compartment. The well was covered by a sliding panel and was only accessible when the fall was in the open position.

Being rather difficult to get at when the open fall was covered with documents its use was abandoned and it had disappeared from the design of most bureaux by 1750.

The charm of many early desks is enhanced by the Georgian love of secret drawers. It is always the fond dream of the antique furniture collector that one day he or she will buy a bureau and, during that first exciting examination when the new piece has been delivered to the house, a hitherto undiscovered secret drawer will be found. Alas! I have never had the luck although a friend once bought a small wooden casket which proved to have a secret drawer and when this was opened after much patient searching for the secret locking device it was found to contain a gold brooch which had lain hidden for nearly 200 years. The remains of a quill pen, jammed in the back of the well, has been the only personal relic of a previous owner which I have ever found in an old desk.

On the whole, secret drawers were seldom as ingeniously secretive as one could have wished. They follow a certain set pattern of variations; the document slides behind the half pillars on the front of the interior compartment; a false bottom to one of the small drawers; a shallow drawer concealed behind part of the shaped border above the pigeon-holes; the drawer behind a drawer which pulls out on a long handle like a church collecting box. I think the best one I have ever come across was the secret drawer which had a false bottom, a sort of double-bluff. I only hope that the designer never felt the vexation of having it burgled.

Large knee-hole desks with flat tops were made about the middle of the 18th century. Some, being very large and double sided, were known as partners' desks. They were so designed that two people could work as they sat facing one another. A smaller version of the knee-hole desk appeared during the early Georgian period and is very much sought after today. One in walnut and in good condition might cost anything up to £200. There is some doubt, however, as to whether these smaller knee-hole desks were actually made to serve as desks or were really designed as small dressing tables. Further reference will be made to this point in the following chapter.

Another type of desk which was made during the later Georgian period was the *secrétaire*. This has all the appearance of being just a chest of drawers but it is recognisable from the outside when it is recalled that the drawers in an ordinary chest become progressively deeper as they near the floor. The deepest drawer of an escritoire is located at the top and is in fact the fall of a desk. When the top section of the chest is pulled out, pressure on catches at either side of the front will allow the false drawer front to fold outwards when it is normally supported by brass stays. The secretaire has the usual fitted interior of small drawers and pigeon-holes and was a favourite form of writing desk until well into the 19th century. The two stage military chest referred to in Chapter 3 sometimes has an escritoire drawer fitted into the upper part.

A number of small desks, intended specifically for the use of ladies, were designed by Sheraton and his contemporaries. They were lightly made and were referred to as boudoir desks or writing tables. Among them was a revival of the smaller desk on a stand which was called a cylinder top desk. Instead of the usual desk-fall it had a curved top which was made to slide backwards to reveal the fitted interior.

Another version was adapted from a French design and was known as a *bonheur du jour*. This is a title for which there is no suitable English equivalent; literally it means "the happiness of the day". As letter writing was one of the chief relaxations of ladies of the more leisured classes in the later 18th century perhaps "bonheur du jour" means just what the name implies.

A little desk known as a davenport was very popular among the Victorians until about 1860. It was supposed to have been first made by Gillows of Lancaster to the design of a Captain Davenport. Early examples were made in mahogany and were rectangular in shape, the desk-top being constructed to slide forward over the knees of the user when required. After 1830 the davenport was usually made in walnut and the desk top was designed to overhang permanently, being supported by carved legs or brackets. Until recently, davenports could be purchased for a few pounds and may still be acquired very reasonably.

Bookshelves have been in use ever since books have been collected into libraries but it was not until the Restoration that the bookcase with glazed doors appeared in this country. Credit for the design is given to the great diarist, Samuel Pepys who was an ardent book-lover. In the Pepys library at Magdalene College, Cambridge, are the original bookcases which Pepys had made for his own use and which he bequeathed with his books to his old university.

At approximately the same time as features of the desk on a stand and the scrutoire were combined to produce the bureau, a bookcase was superimposed on some examples to form the bureau bookcase. It was first made about 1700 and is still being produced in a variety of forms. Some early bureau bookcases had doors fitted with mirrors instead of plain glass. These were fashionable during the Queen Anne period and are very rare today. Some small walnut bureaux with a single mirrored door were made to fit between the long sash windows of the early 18th-century drawing rooms and their value at present might be £700 or £800 each. An interesting feature of the bureaux with mirrors in the doors were the little candlestick slides fitted into the rail just under the doors and above the desk proper. When lighted candles were placed upon them at night the illumination was doubled by the reflected light from the mirrors.

Plain glass doors through which the gilded leather binding of the books could be seen superseded the mirrored doors by 1720. The glazed variety were known as astragal doors from the beading or astragals which formed the framework for the glass. There is a story that all genuine old bookcases have thirteen glazed sections in each door. This would appear to be yet another legend without foundation because I have not infrequently seen genuine old doors with fifteen astragal panels.

Another of the many pieces of furniture which originated during the Restoration was the china cabinet. Collecting the attractive new porcelain from the far east with its translucent body and fine decoration became very popular in London and the larger sea-port towns. To preserve their fragile specimens, lacquered cabinets from China were imported and mounted on heavily carved wooden stands of British manufacture. These were sometimes coated with silver or gilding and were quite a decorative feature of Restoration and William and Mary period furnishing. The fact that the contents of the lacquered cabinets were not visible probably brought about their replacement by the glazed china cabinets of the Queen Anne period. These were usually mounted on a lower stand furnished with the cabriole legs of the times.

For some reason, perhaps because an 18th-century bookcase may be too overpowering in the 20th-century house, it has become the practice in recent years to separate bureaux from their bookcases. The result is that the latter may often be obtained for under £10 and mounted on a small stand or side table they make very attractive china cabinets.

Sets of wall shelves were in use during the 16th and 17th centuries but apart from small racks for holding pewter spoons, few have survived. Small fitments of wall shelves were reintroduced about the middle of the Georgian period. Normally, they consisted of two or three shelves with two small drawers beneath and those of the later Chippendale school had delicately fretted sides. Being very lightly made they could be used only for small books but in all probability they were designed to display ornaments. The later types were of thinly cut mahogany with pleasantly shaped sides and a little boxwood stringing inlaid along the edges of the drawers.

The late Georgian period saw the production of standing bookshelves or bookcases without doors, many made to the designs of Hepplewhite and Sheraton. They were comparatively small, being only about 3 feet in height and width and, as well as being made in mahogany, quite a number were constructed in pine. These were then painted either white or black with gilding and though not particularly common can sometimes be bought quite cheaply at house sales.

17TH AND 18TH-CENTURY DESK

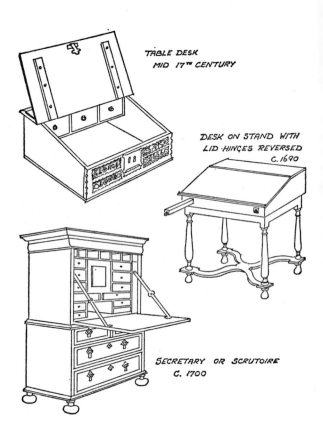

TABLE DESK
MID 17™ CENTURY

DESK ON STAND WITH
LID HINGES REVERSED
C. 1690

SECRETARY OR SCRUTOIRE
C. 1700

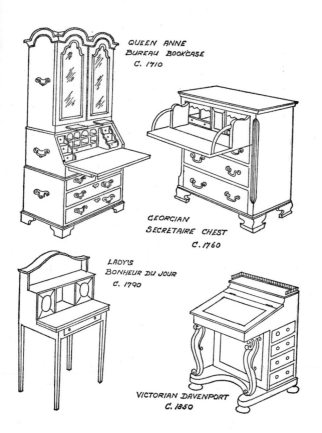

QUEEN ANNE
BUREAU BOOKCASE
C. 1710

GEORGIAN
SECRETAIRE CHEST
C. 1760

LADY'S
BONHEUR DU JOUR
C. 1790

VICTORIAN DAVENPORT
C. 1850

CHINESE LACQUER CABINET ON
CARVED STAND OF ENGLISH
MANUFACTURE C. 1690

MAHOGANY BOOKCASE
WITH ASTRAGAL DOORS
C. 1760

STANDING BOOKCASE
C. 1800

HANGING SHELVES
C. 1775

CHAPTER 9

Dressing Tables, Mirrors and Washstands

Restoration appearance of the dressing table—lowboys and knee-hole dressing tables—tables with fitted interiors—Vauxhall glass and Restoration wall mirrors—development of table mirrors with desk bases—18th-century wall mirrors—the mirror with candle sockets and arms—lightly made washstands of the 18th century.

Small side tables were used as dressing tables prior to the Restoration but were not constructed specifically for this purpose. Even during the latter half of the 17th century small occasional tables with a shallow drawer under the top were used in bedrooms and dressing rooms for holding toilet preparations and hand mirrors. Standing table mirrors had not yet been introduced and rectangular wall mirrors with wide convex frames were hung upon the wall above the tables used for dressing.

It was not until the reign of William and Mary that dressing tables, which were designed for the purpose, appeared on the scene. This type of table is sometimes referred to as a writing table and in America is known as a lowboy. It was constructed with two small drawers above a single, long drawer and usually stood on four cabriole legs. Like most of the furniture of the period it was made in veneered, burr walnut. Some versions had a single, shallow drawer situated under the table top with deeper and narrower drawers at either side. Another class of dressing table which was made about the same time was the knee-hole pattern. This consisted of two nests of small drawers on either side of a recessed cupboard. Any doubt as to whether this piece of furniture might have been designed as a knee-hole desk may be dispelled wherever a pull-out brushing or dressing slide is found immediately under the top.

During the first quarter of the 18th century a further development occurred when the dressing table top was made to open like a chest lid. On the underside a framed rectangular mirror was fitted and the space immediately beneath was divided by partitions into numerous receptacles and boxes for holding cosmetics, pins and all the paraphernalia of the toilet set. The dressing table with the lift-up top and fitted interior continued to be made during the greater part of the long Georgian period, often without any drawers at all. On the other hand, there was a vogue for small chests of drawers, where the top drawer contained a mirror and fitted interior, which would also serve as dressing tables.

In an earlier chapter, mention was made of certain ingenious designs for small articles of furniture which were intended for some particular purpose and among these may be included the *poudreuse*. This was a small dressing table in which a central section of the top opened back to reveal a toilet mirror. On either side of this were two circular lids, let into the table top, which gave access to the powder containers beneath. This was for use in a time when both men and women wore elaborately dressed wigs which were always kept profusely powdered.

Before giving a more detailed description of the types of mirror used during the 17th and 18th centuries, a note on the development of mirror glass production in the British Isles during this time might prove helpful. The manufacture of clear plate glass for mirrors, except in rather small sizes, was not possible before the Restoration. The Duke of Buckingham sponsored the opening of a glassworks at Vauxhall in London about 1665, and a process for making larger sheets of glass was developed here. Because of the method of silvering then in use the makers were unable to produce mirrors of more than 4 feet in length. The thickness of the glass was appreciably less than that of later mirrors and one of the most important characteristics of these early examples was the very slight bevel which was ground on the edges. The steeper and sharper bevel belongs to those mirrors produced during the 19th century or later. Vauxhall glass continued to be made until nearly the end of the Georgian period and mirrors were also manufactured at certain other glass-houses, such as the one at Southwark.

As already mentioned, Restoration mirrors were surrounded with wide, convex framing which is sometimes referred to as *bolection moulding*. The frame was usually veneered with burr walnut, oystershell or flower marquetry. It was not until the later William and Mary period that swing-mirrors mounted on a stand were introduced. These were rectangular in shape with slightly incurving upper corners. They were pivoted on two straight uprights which fitted into a base containing a till of small drawers. A number of these early mirror bases were quite deep and sometimes had the appearance of miniature bureaux.

Later in the 18th century, bases became somewhat more shallow and had flat tops with serpentine or bow fronts which matched the dressing tables or chests of drawers upon which they were designed to stand. The uprights from which the mirror was suspended were also shaped and the mirrors were set in an oval framing or in one of shield or similar form. Towards the end of the century many small standing mirrors were made which had feet but no bases with drawers.

As the 18th century progressed new methods of silvering enabled larger mirrors to be made and these were usually framed in the architectural tradition with a frieze, cornice and pediment above. Those which were made to hang between the long sash windows of the Georgian with-drawing rooms were known as pier glasses. A small side table of similar design was often placed below the mirror or a console table with one elaborate supporting leg in the centre.

Convex mirrors were in favour after the introduction of sideboards in the time of Adam and Hepplewhite. It is said that they were designed to be hung above the side-board so that the butler, without embarrassing the diners by too obviously overlooking, could watch the progress of the meal reflected in the mirror and could more unob-trusively direct his waiting servants in their duties. These convex mirrors with an ebony bezel and deep *cavetto* frames, decorated with a series of small gilded balls, date from those years around the late 18th and early 19th centuries.

The overmantel mirror was another pattern which was becoming more popular during the later Georgian period. It was introduced about 1745 at a time when fireplaces were beginning to be made smaller. This type of mirror was very often designed with three glass panels, one larger central mirror being flanked by two smaller ones. They were frequently produced with architectural embellish-ments in the Adam style and the frieze above the glass carried a conventional design of husks in swags, ribbons and medallions or a low-relief group of classical figures. As the 19th century progressed the overmantel mirror was made in one large sheet of glass which steadily increased in size until it almost filled the entire wall space over the mantelpiece.

Because it was realised that a good reflecting surface would increase the volume of light, many 18th century wall mirrors were equipped with branches and candle sockets. Small mirrors in plain frames with a single candle branch were known as *sconces* while those in elaborately carved and gilded settings of rococo design were called *girandoles* after the French originals. Girandoles were usually of asymmetrical shape but were made in pairs to produce a symmetrical or balanced effect.

Personal cleanliness was not the sort of thing that people of the 17th and 18th centuries worried much about. When the Romans occupied these islands 1500 years earlier, the civilised Britons lived in villas which were well equipped with hot baths and other hygienic amenities. These disappeared after the end of the Roman occupation and were not revived until the reign of Queen Victoria was more than half over.

In Chippendale's time a superficial rinsing of hands and face was all that was considered necessary in the way of daily ablutions. Consequently, mid-Georgian washstands were very lightly made. There were two main types, the first of which was rectangular in shape with a double lid on the top. The water jug and basin were kept in a small cupboard beneath and when required were lifted out and placed in a circular recess in the top, after the lids had been opened.

The second type was even more lightly made and consisted of a rectangular or triangular stand, on the top of which the ewer and basin were placed permanently, but a shelf was provided half-way down on which to stand the jug while the basin was being used. The triangular washstand was designed to fit into a corner and was probably intended for the smaller bedrooms where space might be at a premium. These stands are often employed nowadays as bedside tables, to take a reading lamp and a book. Unfortunately, the original top with the basin hole in it is sometimes replaced. While it is necessary to carry out some modification if the stand is to be used as a table, it is always preferable to leave an antique piece of furniture in its original state. Here the problem may be solved by overlaying a new top on the original one. A third, but much less common type of small wash-basin stand is dealt with in the following chapter.

The introduction of larger jugs and basins made of the new ironstone china in the early 19th century and the growing demand for better washing facilities produced a larger and more strongly made washstand. This was about 3 feet in length with high sides and back to prevent water being splashed around. The top was plain, without a recess for the basin, and there were two drawers underneath with a shelf nearer the floor. These Regency washstands were usually made in mahogany with turned legs. They make very good writing tables as modern bedrooms with running water or an adjacent bathroom render their original purpose obsolete.

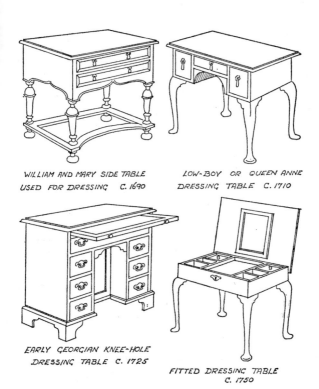

WILLIAM AND MARY SIDE TABLE
USED FOR DRESSING C. 1690

LOW-BOY OR QUEEN ANNE
DRESSING TABLE C. 1710

EARLY GEORGIAN KNEE-HOLE
DRESSING TABLE C. 1725

FITTED DRESSING TABLE
C. 1750

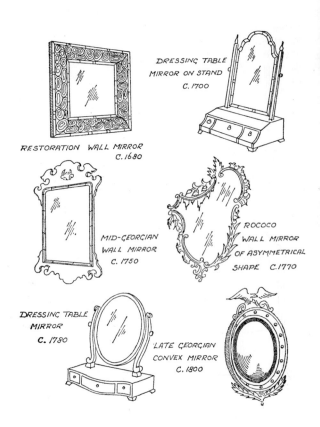

RESTORATION WALL MIRROR
C. 1680

DRESSING TABLE
MIRROR ON STAND
C. 1700

MID-GEORGIAN
WALL MIRROR
C. 1750

ROCOCO
WALL MIRROR
OF ASYMMETRICAL
SHAPE C. 1770

DRESSING TABLE
MIRROR
C. 1780

LATE GEORGIAN
CONVEX MIRROR
C. 1800

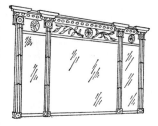

OVERMANTEL MIRROR IN
LATE GEORGIAN CLASSICAL STYLE
C. 1800

WASHSTAND WITH FOLD-OVER
TOP AND MIRROR C. 1760

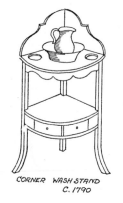

CORNER WASH STAND
C. 1790

EARLY 19TH CENTURY
WASHSTAND FOR THE
LARGER AND HEAVIER
IRONSTONE CHINA
TOILET SETS

CHAPTER 10

Fire-screens and Various Small Stands

Grate screens—pole-screens for the complexion—candle stands and torchères—book-stands and canterburies—fireside footstools—kettle-stands and tea-poys—dumb-waiters and "hearth cats"—wig-stands and "what-nots".

The 18th-century drawing room was well equipped with small pieces of furniture to make life comfortable and convenient for those who were taking their ease. As much of life in winter was spent around the fire and as fuel was cheap and the fire-places large it became rather a difficult matter to arrange how close one could sit near the fire to enjoy the warmth and yet not be scorched.

To solve this problem two types of fire-screens were employed in mid-Georgian times. One design had a large framed panel of glass supported on feet, in the manner of a cheval mirror, and this could be placed between the seated person and the fire so that the brightness of the latter was in no way dimmed but considerable shelter was afforded from the heat. This type of screen usually stood in the hearth when the fire was not burning but did not conceal the empty, blackened fire-place. It therefore became the practice to replace the clear glass panel with one of coloured tapestry on a wooden backing. While this could be used as a shield against the heat it would also serve as a screen, when stood in the hearth, to hide an empty fire-place.

During the second half of the 18th century, another type of fire-screen was developed, known as the pole-screen. This consisted of a vertical rod supported on tripod feet to which a small rectangular or oval screen was attached. This small screen, which usually consisted of a wooden frame containing a glazed piece of tapestry-work or a silk picture, could be adjusted easily to any required height by means of a set-screw. The pole-screen was essentially a piece of feminine furniture and was lightly constructed so that it could be lifted and sited to ward off the heat of the fire from delicate complexions.

Reading and needlework were the two main fireside pastimes and, as the only illumination was furnished by candles, a number of tripod stands or *torchères*, with a small top surrounded by a gallery, or miniature balustrade, were provided in every large drawing room. On these the candelabra could be placed and the gallery surround would prevent them being easily knocked over. Taller and heavier torchères which were not intended to be moved about were produced by the Chippendale school. These were made in the form of mahogany pedestals in the architectural tradition but later, in the time of the classical revival, the design became much lighter and the stands were very decorative and often covered with gilding.

Another reading aid was the adjustable book-stand. This looks like a small tripod table but can be recognised by the ledge along one side of the top for supporting a book. The top may be tilted so that it can be set at any angle and as the central column is telescopic the book could be maintained at any height required.

The book-stand is often found in the company of a *canterbury*, or music rack. In the later years of the 18th century when the low, rectangular pianoforte was to be found in many drawing rooms, this stand was provided for the storage of music sheets. Later in the 19th century and in our own day it has often been employed as a newspaper and magazine rack. This piece of furniture is said to have been named after an archbishop of Canterbury and this may be another instance of the tendency in later Georgian times to name pieces of furniture after their originators. The davenport, the Pembroke and the Sutherland tables are all examples of this practice. However, the term canterbury was applied to other types of stand, apart from those intended to carry music sheets. A tripod stand with a top consisting of a wooden basket at one end and a container with a lid at the other was used to store the table silver temporarily before washing after the meal. It also was referred to as a canterbury.

Footstools were another type of occasional furniture in common use, particularly in those households where the master suffered from gout. In fact a specially designed gout-stool, well upholstered to provide the maximum comfort for the sufferer, was not an uncommon piece of furniture in the Georgian drawing room or library. These small gout-stools, like a child's chair with a low sloping back and a tilted seat, are sometimes wrongly referred to as a type of *prie-dieu*, or kneeling stool.

Circular footstools with beadwork tops which date from the early Victorian period are often to be found in antique shops but the longer, narrow footstools or fender stools are not encountered so frequently. They were probably designed to enable the sitter's feet to be raised above the level of the high brass fenders which were in favour at the end of the 18th century. It is possible to date these fenderstools by the shape of the very short legs which were always characteristic of the period.

Some other small items of furniture were connected with the rite of afternoon tea preparation. Stands similar to the tripod torchère, but with the feet splayed to a wider extent for greater stability, were used for holding the silver spirit kettles or small tea urns. Another small stand was called a tea-poy and consisted of a small veneered box, not unlike a work-box, mounted on a pedestal. The box usually contained two wooden or Sheffield plate tea-caddies and an Irish cut-glass sugar bowl. To discover a tea-poy with all its original contents is a somewhat rare occurence. A fairly common mistake among antique collectors is to refer to those small, rectangular, porcelain tea-containers of the 18th century as tea-poys. This is quite a misnomer as the tea-poy was actually the casket on a stand as already described while the tea-containers were known as caddies.

Two further trappings of the tea party were the dumb-waiter and the "hearth cat". The former consisted of a tripod base supporting a central column on which were mounted two or three circular trays, one above the other. These were made with a slightly raised edge and could be revolved on the column so that the plates of cakes and biscuits could be brought easily within reach of the guests.

There seems to be some doubt as to the actual purpose for which the "hearth cat" was designed. It was called a cat because, no matter how it was moved, it would always fall firmly on three of its six legs or arms. I have heard it referred to as a wig-stand but it could never have been used for that purpose. It was undoubtedly some sort of plate holder but probably not a plate warmer, as it has often been named. The finely turned and polished arms could not have been placed sufficiently near the fire to warm the plates for fear of scorching the wood. Such a device would surely have been made of metal. I think the "hearth cat" was just a stand for holding small trays or plates of food or perhaps for carrying a punch-bowl.

Another little tripod stand which is something of an enigma is one popularly known as a wig-stand. On the top it has a wooden ring and underneath a small shelf with a drawer or two. Immediately above the tripod feet is another small circular tray. It is true that its shape would have supported the fairly full wig of a mid-18th century gentleman but there was actually a small stand specifically designed for hanging a wig on when it was not required. The wig-stand proper has a rounded mushroom shaped top on a baluster stem which fits into a circular base. I have seen the type of stand with the ring top carrying a porcelain bowl and ewer and it was undoubtedly a portable Georgian wash-stand. There are many interesting sources of nomenclature for the keen antiquary to ferret out with regard to old furniture.

Finally, in this miscellany of small stands some mention should be made of the "what-not". This term usually conjures up thoughts of fussy wall-stands of fretted walnut which were used to display some of the bric-à-brac of the Victorian drawing room. In point of fact, the "what-not" originally developed from the French *étagère*. This was a very delicately made buffet type of stand with a shallow drawer under the top or middle shelf which was introduced into this country during the second half of the 18th century. Etagères were designed in the first place as small book-stands but in the early 19th century were used for the display of china ornaments.

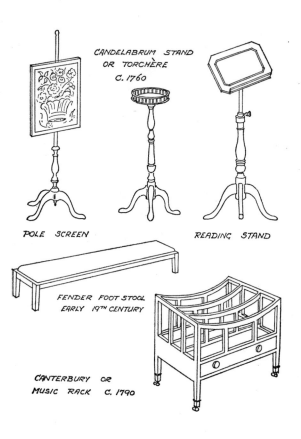

CANDELABRUM STAND
OR TORCHÈRE
C. 1760

POLE SCREEN

READING STAND

FENDER FOOT STOOL
EARLY 19TH CENTURY

CANTERBURY OR
MUSIC RACK C. 1790

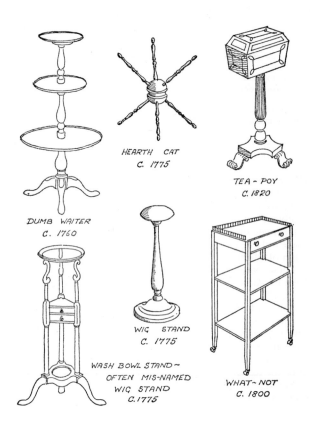

HEARTH CAT
C. 1775

TEA-POY
C. 1820

DUMB WAITER
C. 1760

WIG STAND
C. 1775

WASH BOWL STAND~
OFTEN MIS-NAMED
WIG STAND
C. 1775

WHAT~NOT
C. 1800

126

CHAPTER 11

Wall, Long Case and Table Clocks

Early domestic clocks—the development of the "grandfather" or long case clock—characteristics of case design—some famous makers —telling the age by dial and hands—introduction of white dials— effects of the Industrial Revolution—provincial clockmakers and cottage craftsmen.

The domestic clock was an exceptionally rare possession in the 16th century. It would be reasonable to say that before the Tudor monarchy it was unheard of in the English house. In the painting of Sir Thomas More's family by Holbein, referred to earlier in the book, there is a clock to be seen hanging on the wall next to the dressoir. It is a Gothic clock of probably German origin and was the forerunner of the smaller brass lantern clock which was made only rarely in the British Isles towards the end of the reign of Elizabeth I.

These early clocks were always weight driven, never went for more than 30 hours and were made to hang upon the wall. They were provided with a wrought-iron ring for suspending from a hook and two spurs at the lower part of the back of the clock to keep it in an upright position. The movements, sometimes referred to as the "works", were governed by a balance wheel escapement, as the principle of the pendulum was not applied to clock mechanism until the middle of the 17th century.

Another type of clock which was produced in early times was the brass table clock and this also was an importation from the continent. It was constructed in the form of a square or round box, standing on small feet, the dial situated on the top in a horizontal position like a sun-dial. Consequently it was not possible to ascertain the time from a distance. The table clock was spring driven and while a few English examples were made during the 17th and 18th centuries, production ceased around 1770, apart from those later developed as chronometers.

Clocks in wooden cases, which are really the only kind to be included under the heading of furniture, did not appear until the Restoration, either as mantel clocks or in the form usually referred to as "grandfather". Hitherto, clocks had not been very accurate time-keepers and were often as much as an hour fast or slow in a day. It was the adaptation for clockwork of Galileo's invention of the pendulum by a Dutch scientist named Huygens in 1657 which allowed a considerable improvement in time recording to be made. This coincided with the introduction of wooden clock cases.

A young Londoner, John Fromanteel, had been apprenticed to a Dutch clockmaker at The Hague about this time. He learned the secret of making pendulum clocks and brought it back to England in 1658. The new controlling mechanism was known as a *verge escapement* and the pendulum used was quite short, being about 7 inches in length.

It was shortly after 1660 that the first grandfather clocks appeared in this country. The term "grandfather" is really of late Victorian origin and they were always referred to during the 17th and 18th centuries as long case clocks. Some writers on British horology have attempted to trace the development of the long case clock from the brass lantern type. It is true that after 1660 many lantern clocks were covered over with a wooden hood which had a glazed front. This hood was fitted to a bracket upon which the clock stood and the driving weight hung down on a rope below the movement. Presumably the hood was introduced to keep dust away from the mechanism.

The possibility of damage to the clock by clumsy servants, children or domestic animals interfering with the hanging weight would have been a good reason for its enclosure in a long wooden case. In this way the shape of the long case clock could have been developed. However, it is now well known that hooded and long case clocks both appeared at about the same time and, including the lantern clock, all three types continued in production until quite late in the 18th century. Long case clocks, of course, were made until the middle of Victoria's reign and a few are still produced at the present day.

Mantel clocks appeared on the scene very shortly after the long case type. They were first known as table or bracket clocks, being designed to stand on a side table or wall bracket. It is seldom that a clock is found today with its original wall bracket. When people acquire these early table clocks they often stand them on a mantelpiece where they look far too big and out of place. It was only after the middle of the 18th century that smaller models were made expressly for the mantelshelf. Early table clocks had square brass dials and were housed in ebony veneered cases while those of the early 18th century had the arch dials of the period and walnut and mahogany were used for the cases.

The first long case clocks were of a very attractive size being quite small compared with those produced 150 years later. Because the pendulum was short and did not extend down into the case, the latter could be made comparatively narrow, often as little as 9 inches in width and very seldom over 6 feet in height. The more expensive clocks had ebony veneered cases and the hoods were designed in a pleasingly plain architectural style, usually with some gilded brass ornaments attached to the pediment and hood framework. The base was surrounded by a simple plinth. These very early long case clocks are exceedingly rare and when they do appear on sale the price is usually in the neighbourhood of £1,000.

During the next 30 years some important changes took place in long case design. Around 1670 a longer pendulum was introduced with a beat of one second. This was a purely English invention and was to revolutionise methods of accurate time-keeping. As the new 39-inch pendulum had an extended swing a slightly wider and taller case became necessary. By 1690 long case clocks had an average height of just under 7 feet and the width varied between 10 and 11 inches. The ebony veneered or ebonised pine cases of the earlier period must have appeared rather sombre when the clocks increased in size because the more colourful burr walnut veneer and flower marquetry cases had displaced them by the end of the century. The pediment on the clock hood was replaced with a carved cresting, pegged into the front edge of the flat top. This is rarely present nowadays as, being easily detached, it was liable to be mislaid during a removal of furniture. The hood, which hitherto had been constructed with a glass panel in front and which had to be lifted upwards when access to the hands was required, now had a glazed door fitted instead.

It also became the practice at this time to insert a little circular or oval window, known as a *lenticle*, in the door of the long case at the height of the pendulum bob. This was intended to show to an observer across the room that the clock was in motion. The gleam of the brass bob as it swung backwards and forwards could be seen clearly from a distance. Originally the lenticle was made of plain glass but in many cases this has been replaced with a piece of thick green glass commonly known as a bull's eye.

Other features of long case clocks at the end of the Restoration were spiral twist pillars fitted to the edges of the hood door and a wide *ovolo* moulding placed immediately below the hood. By 1710 this had been altered to a cavetto shape and the use of the ovolo moulc'ing was never revived. Except in a few instances of country manufacture the small bull's eye windows also became obsolete at about the same time.

Around 1720 long case clocks began to appear with dials surmounted by an arch. This necessitated a taller hood and the case was made higher still by the addition of a moulded or cushion top. The arch of the hood door was matched by a rounded top similar to the trunk door which hitherto had always been rectangular in shape. Cases were also becoming wider and 12 or 13 inches was not an uncommon size. Pillars were still attached to the hood doors but were no longer in the form of spiral twists, being usually plain or fluted columns with brass bases and capitals. During the next 80 years pillars ceased to be placed on the doors but remained free-standing on either side of the hood. A characteristic of Scottish clocks was the retention of the spiral twist pillars in a rather attenuated form until nearly the end of the century.

By 1765 clock cases had reached a height of 7 feet 6 inches or thereabout and had an average width of 14 inches. Mahogany was in general use and the long veneered case doors were often finely figured. While simple wainscot oak versions of the more elaborately veneered London clocks had always been made in the provinces many were now being made in the counties of Lancashire and Yorkshire which were cross-banded with mahogany.

London clocks still maintained a pre-eminence in good design during the latter half of the 18th century but many of the more northerly types were becoming very large indeed. Along with the other pieces of furniture whose design was affected by architectural influences, the broken pediment on the hood was introduced and this in turn developed into the swan-neck pediment. In some cases towards the end of the century the swan-necks became so debased in shape as to appear just like a pair of horns or ears protruding from the top of the hood.

During the early years of the 19th century some rather clumsy long case clocks were being made in the industrial north. Sometimes double sets of pillars appeared on either side of the hood and these on occasion lost any semblance of their architectural origin, becoming merely uninteresting turned spindles. The trunk door had gradually dwindled in size to a small, almost square trap, looking for all the world like the door of a small food larder. As a matter of fact, I have seen very attractive looking small cocktail cabinets, made to hang on the wall, which had been produced from the centre part of the trunks of these large clocks. The craftsmanship of early 19th-century cases was of the highest order but the overall design, generally speaking, was in very poor taste. Such clocks were portents of those monstrosities in furniture design which the Victorians, on occasion, were later to perpetrate.

One of the many interesting characteristics of the long case clocks was that in nearly every instance the name of the maker and place of manufacture were engraved upon the dial. Only in very few examples are clocks found to be anonymous. The earliest of the British clockmakers of whom records are known were probably Nicholas Vallin and Bartholomew Newsam who worked in London towards the end of the reign of Elizabeth I. When James I came from Scotland to become king of England he brought with him a Scottish clockmaker, David Ramsay. The latter was a great clockmaker and became the first Master of the Clockmakers Company which was founded in 1631, during the reign of Charles I. The Stuart kings were all clock lovers and it was largely due to the enthusiasm of Charles II and his great interest in scientific matters that clockmaking in England by the end of the 17th century had become pre-eminent in all Europe. All the makers already mentioned, however, were producers of metal clocks and preceded the era of the clocks in wooden cases.

Ahasuerus Fromanteel, a relation of that John who introduced the pendulum into British clockmaking, was one of the first names to appear on the dial of a long case clock. He was followed during the next 40 years by such famous makers as Edward East, Henry Jones, Thomas Tompion, Joseph Knibb, Daniel Quare and Joseph Windmills. The last I include in this list of the immortals for two reasons. In the first place, he is credited with the introduction of the arch dial in clock design during the first quarter of the 18th century and secondly, I am fortunate to possess a clock in a bird and flower marquetry case of around 1690 made by Joseph Windmills. He was made a member of the Clockmakers Company in 1671, the same year in which Tompion was elected, was Master in 1703 and retired or died in 1740.

There are several sources of information giving details of the early clockmakers such as G. H. Baillie's *Watch-makers and Clockmakers of the World*; F. J. Britten's *Old Clocks and Watches and their Makers* (Revised 7th Edition); John Smith's *Old Scottish Clockmakers* and Iorwith Peate's *Clock and Watch Makers in Wales*. So far there has not been a book written on the Irish makers but many of their names are included in Baillie and Britten.

While the general shape of antique clock cases will give an approximate idea of the period in which they were made it must be remembered that, as with all the furniture styles, what was fashionable in London for a decade continued to be produced in the provinces for another 20 or 30 years in many instances. The details of clock dials and hands, however, give a much closer date approximation.

Early dials were seldom more than 9 inches square but by 1775, 14 inches was not an uncommon size. Until the last quarter of the 18th century all dials had a chapter ring, which bears the hour numerals, and ornamental corner spandrels attached to the dial as separate items. Roman numerals were always used for the hours until after 1800 and above them were engraved Arabic figures. In the 17th century the Arabic numerals were about $\frac{1}{8}$th of the size of the Roman but they were gradually enlarged so that by 1770 they were often $\frac{2}{3}$rds of the size of the latter.

The spandrels were cast in brass and in early clocks were finely chased and gilded. Between 1670 and 1680 a finely modelled but simple cupid's head was fashionable. By 1690 further decorative motifs were added to this pattern and around 1700 the cupid head design was replaced by a bearded mask or a maiden's head surrounded by still more elaborate decoration. A theme of flowers in a vase with seashells was popular about 1740 and during the 1770's the spandrels evolved into an arrangement of rococo arabesques without any realistic representation. In the north about this time there was a revival of the cupid head spandrel but it was much larger than the 17th-century version and appears rather crude when compared with the much finer castings of a hundred years previously.

All domestic clocks before 1660 had only one hand which told the hours and the quarters. More detailed time recording was not considered necessary in those far off and less complicated days. A minute hand was added to some movements early in the Restoration period and a second hand, called a second minute hand, about 1675. In the provinces, nevertheless, country clocks of 30 hours going duration and with only one hand continued in production even as late as 1780 or thereabouts. There seems to have been a dislike for change among the country people who preferred the older and simpler method of time-keeping.

This fact has proved very misleading to many clock owners who think that because a clock has only one hand it must be of an earlier date than 1700 at least.

White dials for long case clocks did not appear before 1775. The earliest were made of fine enamel but these are rare and very soon they were being produced with a painted front. Apart from being much cheaper to manufacture than the engraved brass dial there was the important fact that it was much easier to tell the time from a white dial. The engraving of brass dials towards the end of the 18th century had tended to be much too elaborate and what with hour, minute, centre-second hands and often a calendar indicator all pivoted at the dial centre plus a mass of engraving and over-elaborate spandrels, it became virtually impossible to ascertain the time unless one was standing very close to the clock. White dials for bracket clocks were introduced at the same time as those for the long case variety. In fact, the characteristics of hands, spandrels, chapter rings, etc. followed the same pattern for both types of clock.

The early years of the Industrial Revolution had a considerable effect on the production of clock dials and movements. Although the distribution of goods was still a very slow and arduous matter in the late 18th century, the pack-horse was capable of transporting clock dials, trains of wheels and most of the parts which went to make up a clock movement, to the most out-of-the-way villages in the country. For this reason there exists a marked similarity between late Georgian clocks although they may have been made over quite a large area of the country. The country clockmaker had, in fact, become a mere assembler of parts and no longer constructed the entire clock by hand in his own workshop as he had done earlier in the century.

A feature of 18th-century clockmaking was the very considerable amount of repetition work which was performed in the cottage homes of specialist craftsmen such as the clock-hand maker. In many cases their wives and children assisted in the work. Chains for *fusee movements*, the filing and gilding of spandrels after casting, the engraving of dials and many other particular processes were performed on a small bench at home and taken weekly to the master-clockmaker, who with his assistants would assemble the movement.

The wooden long cases and also those for the bracket clocks were not made by the clockmaker but by an outside craftsman who specialised in the work. Thus it is that in some instances clocks made by well-known contemporaries like Tompion, Quare, Knibb and Windmills are found in cases which have identical marquetry designs and other features which indicate that they must have originated in the same workshops. Cases for country clocks were usually made by local joiners and like other examples of country-made furniture exhibit a certain naïvety in their appearance.

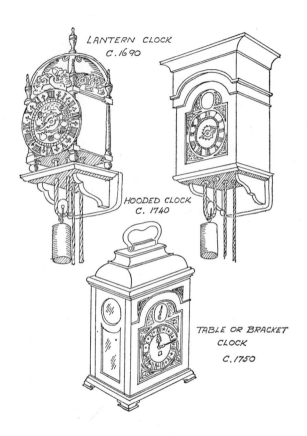

LANTERN CLOCK
C. 1690

HOODED CLOCK
C. 1740

TABLE OR BRACKET
CLOCK
C. 1750

RESTORATION
C. 1670

WILLIAM AND MARY
C. 1690

EARLY GEORGIAN
C. 1725

MID-GEORGIAN
C. 1765

LATE GEORGIAN
C. 1790

NORTH COUNTRY
C. 1820

CHAPTER 12

Restoring and Preserving Antique Woodwork

Methods of removing old varnish—preservation of patina—various
polishes—repairs to inlay and cross-banding—troubles with veneers
—new runners for drawers—replacement of handles—woodworm
and precautions against it—dangers of central heating—use of
humidifiers—upholstery repairs and renovation—some points to
look for when buying—fakes and forgeries.

The best work of the early cabinet-makers was hand
polished with oil and wax but much old furniture of the
17th and 18th centuries was coated with varnish. Like
the varnish on old oil-paintings, this deteriorates with
time into a cracked, semi-opaque, yellowish film which
completely conceals the natural beauty of the wood. Some
people advocate the sponging of furniture with warm
water, linseed oil and vinegar but it should be appreciated
that water should never be applied to old woodwork.
Timber which is more than a century old is usually very
dry and tends to absorb moisture to a considerable
extent. Consequently, a certain amount of swelling would
take place which could make drawers stick and might
even cause warping and twisting.

I have always found that very fine wire-wool will remove
old varnish quite easily. It should be rubbed carefully
in the direction of the grain and not across it in order to
avoid scratching the surface. If the varnish is very thick
or if the piece of furniture has been painted then a proprie-
tary paint-stripper is more effective. In the directions for
use on the container, water is sometimes recommended
for removing the softened paint but if turpentine substitute

or methylated spirit is used instead, then no harm can come to the old wood.

Patina on old furniture is the effect produced by years of waxing, polishing and much tender care. It is something much more than the glassy finish of Victorian French polish and it has an elegant, antique charm of its own. It cannot be replaced when once removed and second thoughts are always advisable before going to work on the cleaning of old woodwork.

After the removal of the varnish, the wood should be lightly rubbed with a small cloth pad dipped in linseed oil. This will help to restore the colour and the nature of the timber. Leave this to dry out for a day or two, then apply a thin coat of white shellac polish with a camel hair mop-brush. After allowing it to dry thoroughly, rub the surface very lightly with a very fine grade glasspaper. A good wax polish should then be applied and after a little rubbing, a surface with a suggestion of patina will begin to appear.

Where the woodwork is well carved, shoe-brushes are invaluable for polishing right into the crevices of the carving. Blacking brushes must not be used, of course, and for the lighter woods it is better to wash the brushes first. Dark tan shoe-polish is very effective for giving new life to old mahogany when it has faded badly. Exposure to sunlight over a period of years will cause it to lose a lot of its colour but this may be restored by the method just described. The old polish must first be removed to enable the dark tan polish to be brushed well into the grain.

It is not uncommon to find that small pieces of inlay and cross-banding are missing from the edges of table tops and drawer fronts. Veneers are usually sold in large sheets but it is possible to buy small pieces to match the missing parts from "hobby" or handicraft shops where they sell it for making marquetry pictures. Prior to the 19th century veneers were cut with a saw and are about twice the thickness of those used at the present day. It will be necessary, therefore, to cut a double thickness to fill the vacant space or to saw a small piece of veneer of the required size from an old piece of the same type of wood. Powdered resin glue is best for these light repair jobs as a very small amount can be easily and quickly mixed with a little cold water in an old egg-cup. When glued in position the new piece of cross-banding can be held down firmly with a couple of strips of plastic adhesive tape.

Veneers which have lifted slightly may be damped, glued down and held flat with a weight. Where the veneer has rippled, because the foundation wood has shrunk, the repair is a task for an expert cabinet-maker. If the old veneer cannot be partly lifted and relaid without damage then it is better to leave it than have it replaced by new veneer.

Old drawers are sometimes very worn under the side linings and it is quite a legitimate repair to have these restored by fixing new runners. If possible old wood should be used to complete the repair. It is seldom that all the handles on a chest of drawers are original as the tugging and pulling of centuries are bound to have broken some and replacements will have been made. If there are any old established firms of cabinet-makers in your neighbourhood they might be able to supply you with original old handles. Reproduction brass handles can be obtained from any large ironmongers or from advertisers in the antiques periodicals. The general shape and characteristics of the chest should indicate the period of the handles required.

The Victorians had an unfortunate habit of replacing 18th-century brass handles with turned wooden knobs.

The twin holes where the original handle was fixed can usually be discerned on either side of the wooden knob but it must also be remembered that not a few early Victorian bow-front chests with traces of Georgian influence in their design have had the original wooden knobs removed and these have been replaced with Regency style brass reproduction handles.

The majority of pieces of antique furniture show some sign of bygone woodworm activity but unless the holes are freshly made and there are traces of wood powder it is usually safe to assume that the woodbeetles have long since flown. It is always a wise safeguard to give a coating of one of the better known woodworm insecticides to the interior of any recently acquired piece of old woodwork. On the other hand, it is possible to prepare a home-concocted and very effective woodworm preventive by dissolving $\frac{1}{4}$lb of para-dichlor-benzine crystals in 1 pint of turpentine substitute or paraffin oil. The crystals may be obtained from the gardening department of any large chemists. This is a very penetrating solution and is a preparation used in many museums and art galleries where there are collections of antique furniture.

One of the chief hazards to old woodwork in the modern home is central heating. The dry atmosphere can play havoc with pieces which have survived for centuries and particularly with those which have been veneered. I have seen the fall of a Georgian bureau and the top of an envelope card table warp and twist to a distressing degree. Some museums take the precaution of using portable humidifiers which send an invisible cloud of fine water spray into the atmosphere. These machines are rather expensive and can only be justified where the collection of furniture is of considerable importance.

I know of one antique dealer whose show-rooms are always adorned with the most beautiful flower arrangements, set in large bowls. Actually, as far as he is concerned, the most important part of the display is the capacity of the flower bowls which are always kept well filled with water. These are very successful in counteracting any ill effects from his efficient central heating system. One long oak table, which had developed a hump in the middle through being too close to a radiator, regained its normal shape after a large flower bowl had been placed beneath it for a few days.

Replacement of upholstery on chairs and settees is always a legitimate restoration so long as the original covering is in a very worn condition and has no outstanding merit in itself. Should the fabric be late 18th-century Aubusson tapestry, specially woven for the set of chairs or just early Hungarian point woolwork, then expert opinion should be sought to find out whether the original material can be repaired or protected by a transparent oiled silk covering. Otherwise, there is nothing to be said for having a beautiful 18th-century chair which is just a mass of rags and tatters.

When you have decided that a few pieces of antique furniture in your home would make for a more gracious way of living, do not start by purchasing the first article which takes your fancy, unless you are absolutely sure of what you are doing. Most collectors are prepared to write off the cost of a misguided purchase as experience which must be paid for, but it is not really necessary to learn the hard way. Your first piece of furniture should preferably be something small and inexpensive which will not disappoint and will stimulate your interest for the more important things to come. Seek a personal introduction to a knowledgeable antique dealer who has a reputation for fair trading. Be prepared to be guided by him until you acquire sufficient knowledge to make a judgment of your own. Do not worry him unduly but tell him what you want and the limit you are prepared to pay. Sooner or later he will find what you are looking for.

Purchasing furniture at a house sale or in an auction room can be a chancy business although I have had some lucky experiences in this respect. Objects are difficult to examine properly in a crowded sale room and it is not easy to decide how *right* a thing is when time may be short and other people are pressing around. Then, when the sale has started anyone may become afflicted with that terrible frenzy to possess a certain lot at all costs. As the auctioneer's hammer falls sanity returns and you realise that you have paid far more than you ever intended. Always set yourself a definite limit on any lot before the sale starts and then if the bidding goes beyond that amount, quietly withdraw and let the others fight it out. The careful buyer will get the deepest satisfaction in the end. In the early stages of collecting, I would strongly advocate buying at antique and second-hand furniture shops where you have time to consider the price and examine the object of your desire thoroughly.

Another very important factor to take into account, when buying old furniture, is the matter of size. Many years ago, I was tempted to purchase a 4 feet long mahogany bureau of the Hepplewhite period. It was a great bargain—and it could also have been a great nuisance. In the large airy store behind the dealer's shop, the bureau looked just the thing I had been looking for. Luckily, I had accepted the dealer's kind offer to have it taken home on approval, to see how it looked in the room at home where it was supposed to go. How glad I was to be able to have it put right back into the carrier's van as soon as it had been brought into the house, because it filled the room and dwarfed everything else in it. For the cost of the cartage in two directions I had learned a valuable lesson and now I always measure up the space available for an intended buy and I carry a 6 foot steel tape measure whenever I go in search of antique furniture.

Some dealers are inclined to be a little vague at times when discussing the authenticity of their wares. I remember paying a visit with a friend to an antique shop in a small south country town. We were looking for an early 17th-century oak armchair and when a specimen was shown to us, we had serious doubts about its antecedents. There were many signs which suggested that it had been "made up", so we asked the dealer how genuine it was.

"Oh! Its genuine all right," he said. Then he gave the game away when he produced a second chair and announced with some pride, "Now, this one is very genuine!"

We did not make a purchase at that shop.

At a sale in London, in the autumn of 1963, a beautiful and perfectly genuine *poudreuse* was sold for £16,000. If a forger was clever enough, it would be worth his while to attempt to reproduce such a piece with intent to deceive. As far as the ordinary collector is concerned, whose purchases are going to be around the £25 to £50 mark, the forger would have little return for his efforts. On the other hand a plain piece of antique furniture might appear more attractive to the innocent—and ignorant—if it was "faked up" a little by the addition of some carving or other ornamentation.

Here then is the difference. The forger counterfeits an antique while the faker alters an inferior but genuine article to make it look like something better. I once saw a rare Stuart stool which a friend of mine had bought. It had been a broken chair from which the back had been sawn and the stumps rounded over, but it took an expert to detect the fake. The feet of tripod tables and the plain knees of early cabriole legs have been adorned, a couple of hundred years after they were made, with carved acanthus leaves or scallop shells. Original carving stands out in relief because the old maker allowed for it when shaping his wood. The modern faker has to incise his carving and it shows below the level of the original surface.

One of the greatest hazards which faces the collector who is not yet well acquainted with his subject is the reproduction article, made as a wholesome, undisguised reproduction about sixty years ago. By now it will have received a certain amount of rubbing and wear and it would take a close and knowledgeable scrutiny to identify it for what it was. If you look at advertisements in pre-1914 copies of magazines about antiques you will see that well-known furniture makers advertised reproduction Tudor and Stuart furniture made "entirely from Old Oak". One such advertisement from the year 1906 showed a number of illustrations of chairs and chests which were excellent copies. In another paper was the picture of an oak chest which had on it a large Staffordshire, earthenware mug. Under the picture was the legend, "A mug for 6 shillings". I am not sure to this day, whether the advertisement referred to the actual piece of pottery or to the person who was going to buy it.

CHAPTER 13

Some Woods used by the Furniture Makers

Amboyna — Ash — Beech — Birch — Boxwood — Cedar — Chestnut — Deal — Ebony — Elm — Holly — Kingwood — Laburnum — Lime — Mahogany — Maple — Mulberry — Oak — Olive — Rosewood — Sabicu — Satinwood — Thuya — Tulipwood — Walnut — Yew — Zebrawood.

AMBOYNA is a hard and very durable wood of a light, warm brown colour tending to orange. It was imported from the island of Amboyna in the East Indies and was used by many of the better type cabinet-makers during the 18th century. It has an attractive, wavy, burr-like grain which makes it very suitable for veneering and inlay work. As supplies of the wood began to be exhausted during the 19th century, it was gradually replaced by thuya from North Africa.

ASH is found generally distributed throughout Europe and when employed in country-made antique furniture it is usually of British origin. It is a very light-straw coloured wood with a grain resembling that of oak but without the figuring or silver grain. The outstanding characteristic of ash is its elasticity which enables it to be bent or set in almost any shape. For this reason the hoops on the backs of Windsor chairs are often made of ash and it was always employed in the manufacture of the wooden parts of agricultural implements. Like chestnut, ash was sometimes pollarded or cut down so that the sawn-off stump would sprout and produce long shoots for use as bean or hop-poles. Because of the burr formations in the grain obtained by the pollarding, the tree-bole was sometimes sawn into veneers. These were seldom used in the better class furniture.

BEECH has always been the most popular wood with the chair-maker and the turner. Its colour varies from a grey-pink to a warm yellow, according to the district in which it is grown. The timber has an even grain which is hard, straight and free from knots but it is not interesting from a decorative point of view. It is a native of the British Isles and in some areas like the Chiltern Hills, where there are extensive beech forests, furniture making and turning have become long established, traditional crafts. Beech is very liable to attack by woodworm and as it was much used in the past for the seat-framing of chairs which were subsequently covered with upholstery, the pest was able to continue its ravages unobserved.

BIRCH, like beech, is a close-grained timber of a grey-white colour. It is found in most European countries and the timber has been used extensively in the manufacture of country-type furniture. It is not usually affected by woodworm and as it has a finely lined, wavy grain it can be mistaken for mahogany when stained. It has also been used as a cheap substitute for satinwood. For centuries, birch has been used by turners all over Europe and many antique bowls and platters are found made of this wood. In modern times, plywood has been manufactured to a great extent from birch.

BOXWOOD is probably the most solid and densely grained of all European hardwoods. It has a pleasant golden-yellow colour and in the past has been much used for inlaid work. In Tudor and early Stuart times it was employed for geometric and flower patterns in conjunction with bog oak and holly; after the Restoration for marquetry and parquetry designs and in the later Georgian period for insets and edge stringing on mahogany furniture. Box has always been a favourite material with woodcarvers and sculptors like Grinling Gibbons. Wood engravers have also used it extensively for print making, and long established periodicals like the *Illustrated London News* used boxwood engraved illustrations until quite late in the 19th century.

CEDAR is the name given to a large family of brown coloured, evenly grained timbers which are not native to the British Isles but which have been imported for centuries from the

Middle East, India and the West Indies. Of these, the Lebanon cedar is probably the best known. It has been used since ancient times because of its heavily perfumed wood which has always been considered repellent to obnoxious insects. The strong, incense-like scent of cedar is very persistent as those who have visited the chapel at Chatsworth House in Derbyshire will recall. Here, the cedar panelling was installed towards the end of the 17th century and today, over 250 years later, the atmosphere is full of the spicy smell of the wood. Another form of cedar closely resembles a light coloured, rather open-grained mahogany and this was used extensively for drawer linings in the late 18th century.

CHESTNUT is a widely grown forest tree of the British Isles and the wood of the horse chestnut variety was used in country-made furniture for chairs, stools, tables and drawer linings. The sweet chestnut has a pleasing, reddish-brown grain of an open, well-marked character. The wood can be obtained in wide boards and was used for table tops and the carcasses of chests of drawers. Unfortunately, it was very susceptible to attack by woodbeetle and antique furniture made of this wood should be the subject of close scrutiny.

DEAL is the generic term applied to a large number of soft-wood timbers. Originally a deal was a measured quantity of pine-wood and the importer still trades in deals of timber. Northern pine is grown in many European countries and when sawn into boards is known as red or yellow deal according to the colour. Deal has always been used to a considerable degree in the manufacture of furniture and particularly for cabinets, chests and bureaux which were designed to have a japanned finish. It was also used for furniture and panelling which was to be painted and in cases where the old paintwork has become cracked and unsightly, the practice of stripping the paint off and leaving the deal with a wax-polished surface in a natural colour has become very fashionable during the last few years.

EBONY with its rich black, even grain has been prized as a decorative wood for many centuries. Like boxwood, it is only obtainable in small sizes but its weight would make it impossible to use in the solid. Accordingly, ebony is used as a veneer except for very small objects and the best of the early long-case and bracket clocks were made with ebony veneered on pine. As ebony had to be imported from the East and was a rare and expensive wood it was not unusual to find that a veneer of pearwood, dyed black, was used as a substitute during the 18th century.

ELM is another of the great trees which are native to the British Isles. Its size made it suitable for converting the timber into wide boards which were very durable and resistant to damp conditions. The grain of elm is not unlike that of chestnut or some varieties of oak but it has no figuring in it. It is often of a twisted nature which makes it difficult to work and formerly was only used in the more unsophisticated types of cottage furniture. It has been used traditionally for making the adze-hewn seats of Windsor chairs but, unfortunately, it is often attacked by woodworm. The nature of the tree in producing clumps of sprouting twigs on the side of the trunk provides interesting burr effects when the timber is sawn. Burr-elm was used for cross-banding on oak and as a veneer on some small pieces of country furniture.

HOLLY, when properly seasoned, is the whitest of all our native woods and being hard and close-grained, has been used since early times for inlaid decorative work and for turning. For marquetry designs, holly was often stained green to produce a natural effect of foliage.

KINGWOOD is an attractively coloured hardwood with light and dark purple-brown markings in the grain. It belongs to the rosewood family and as it had to be imported from the Spanish possessions in South America during the 17th century, its rarity and pleasing appearance caused it to be named kingwood. It was used as a veneer on the very best kind of cabinet work produced during the later years of the Restoration and in the William and Mary period.

LABURNUM is probably better known as a small, spring-flowering tree in suburban gardens. Actually, it is the only tree which grows in any profusion in the British Isles whose timber most nearly approaches the quality of those more exotic woods which have always had to be imported from foreign parts. It has a hard, dense grain with a rich, dark-brown heartwood and a light-yellow sapwood. It was used extensively towards the end of the 17th century for oystershell veneering and parquetry work.

LIME was probably the most popular wood used by woodcarvers during the 17th and 18th centuries. Its pale yellow, even grain presented no complication in working and much of the elaborate carving of the Restoration period was carried out in lime. It has been said that Grinling Gibbons could carve flowers and lace cravats in lime which were even more lovely than the real thing. Unfortunately, this timber also was liable to woodworm infestation and many masterpieces of the woodcarver's art have been lost to posterity for this reason.

MAHOGANY *See* Chapter 2.

MAPLE was known in medieval times when it was considered to be a great rarity. Its hard, finely mottled wood made it suitable for turning and large drinking goblets, known as *mazers*, with silver rims and bases which were very much prized. It was also used occasionally during the 17th and 18th centuries as a material for marquetry and inlay but it was not until the early Victorian period that *bird's eye* maple became really popular. This was the sugar maple of North America and its attractive golden colour when polished and the lustrous grain profusely mottled with numerous small knots gave it the name of bird's eye. When cut into veneers, it was used as the lining for davenport desks, walnut sewing tables and the maple picture frames so beloved by the mid-Victorians.

MULBERRY is a rare wood but occasionally pieces of furniture like small bureaux and early clock-cases appear to have been veneered with it. It has a reddish-brown, interesting grain which is hard, close and takes a good polish. The mulberry tree is a native of China and was introduced into Europe in the 15th century.

OAK *See* Chapter 2.

OLIVEWOOD was one of the more unusual timbers used in

antique woodwork. It was employed as a veneer during the latter years of the 17th century, much in the same way as mulberry. It has a greenish-yellow colour and a grain not unlike that of walnut with some darker markings. Olivewood was imported from the Mediterranean countries.

ROSEWOOD is found in a number of varieties, some of which come from Brazil and Central America while others are obtained from India and the far East. One of the species, known as the Jacaranda tree, emits a sweet perfume like the scent of rosewater when it is sawn or planed. Much late-Georgian furniture of the early 19th century was made from rosewood and in spite of its weight it was sometimes used in the solid for chairs and small stands.

SABICU is a dark, reddish-brown wood with an attractive grain. It is very strong, heavy and durable and in the second half of the 18th century was sometimes used as a substitute for mahogany. The staircases at Crystal Palace, which was built for the Great Exhibition of 1851, were made of this wood.

SATINWOOD was imported from India and Ceylon. (*See* Chapter 2.)

SYCAMORE, when properly seasoned, is almost pure white. It is a wood which has long been used for the turning of bowls and other table utensils. It was also employed in place of holly for inlay and marquetry patterns. For centuries it has always been much in demand as one of the woods used in the manufacture of violins. The grain of sycamore with its undulating sheen is often referred to as *fiddle-back*. In the Regency period sycamore was sometimes cut into veneers and dyed a silvery-grey shade when it was known as *harewood*.

THUYA is a sweet smelling wood with a rich brown, burr-mottled grain which is similar to amboyna. It was imported from North Africa and used for the most part as a decorative veneer.

TULIPWOOD has a beautifully striped grain with alternating light-yellow and reddish-brown markings. It was imported from Brazil in the 18th and 19th centuries and was much used as a veneer, for inlay and for cross-banding.

WALNUT *See* Chapter 2.

YEW is a much prized wood when found in old furniture. It has a warm, rich brown grain and acquires a fine patina after years of polishing. Although it was the traditional wood from which the famous English long-bows were made it was also used extensively for turnery and for cutting into veneers. Apart from boxwood and laburnum it is probably one of the heaviest and most dense of British timbers.

ZEBRAWOOD is a generic name applied to many hardwoods with a striped grain which were imported from Central America. It was used largely for veneered furniture in the second half of the 18th century.

APPENDIX

Periods and Dates

EARLY TUDOR	1480–1560.	Henry VII, 1485–1509.
		Henry VIII, 1509–47.
ELIZABETHAN	1560–1600.	Elizabeth I, 1558–1603.
EARLY STUART	1600–1650.	James I, 1603–25.
		Charles I, 1625–49.
		Renaissance influence.
COMMONWEALTH	1650–1660.	Puritan influence.
RESTORATION	1660–1690.	Charles II, 1660–85.
		French and Portuguese influences.
WILLIAM AND MARY	1690–1700.	William III, 1688–1702.
		Dutch influence.
QUEEN ANNE	1700–1720.	Queen Anne, 1702–14.
		Pure English style emerges.
EARLY GEORGIAN	1720–1750.	George I, 1714–27.
		George II, 1727–60.
		School of Wm. Kent. Repeal of mahogany tax, 1733.

MID-GEORGIAN	1750–1790.	George III, 1760–1820. Schools of Thos. Chippendale (*Director* 1754), Robt. Adam (Syon House1762), G. Hepplewhite (*Guide* 1788). Further French influence.
LATE GEORGIAN	1790–1840.	School of Thos. Sheraton (*Drawing Book* 1803). Regency 1811–20.
EARLY VICTORIAN	1840–1860.	Queen Victoria crowned, 1837. The Great Exhibition, 1851.

The dates allotted to the periods are a matter of opinion as fashions cannot be said to have started or ended in any particular year.

The names of Edward VI, Mary Tudor, James II, George IV and William IV are not usually assigned to period lists as there were no important innovations in furniture design during their reigns.

It is accepted that furniture of a Georgian character continued to be made during the first 10 years of Victoria's reign and that the rococo designs in walnut covered a period from approximately 1850 to 1870.

Index

*The asterisked page numbers * refer to illustrations*